TUKWILA SCHOOL DISTRICT 406
4640 South 144th Street
Tukwila, Washington 98168

In the U.S.A.™

Program Authors
Lada Kratky
Deborah J. Short
Josefina Villamil Tinajero

NATIONAL
GEOGRAPHIC

Hampton-Brown

Reviewers

We gratefully acknowledge the many contributions of the following dedicated educators in creating a program that is pedagogically sound, clear and easy to teach, and appealing and appropriate for newcomers.

Jean Anderson
ESOL Curriculum Specialist
Broward County Public Schools
Fort Lauderdale, FL

LaTisha Bard
New Arrival Center Curriculum Coach
Cypress-Fairbanks Independent
School District
Houston, TX

Renee Davis
Secondary ESL Coordinator
Irving Independent School District
Irving, TX

Lynne Fykes Gadbury
ELL/Bilingual Specialist, K-12
Vancouver Public Schools
Vancouver, WA

Brenda Garcia
ESL Teacher
Crockett Middle School
Irving, TX

Aimee Luter, NBCT
Academic Coach
Munsey Elementary School
Bakersfield, CA

Carrie Lutke
ESOL Teacher
Pleasant Valley Middle School
Wichita, KS

Laurie Manikowski
ELD Teacher/Instructional Coach
Lee Matheson Middle School
San Jose, CA

Rebecca Varner
ELL Teacher
Copley-Fairlawn Middle School
Copley, OH

Acknowledgments

Grateful acknowledgment is given to the authors, artists, photographers, museums, publishers, and agents for permission to reprint copyrighted material. Every effort has been made to secure the appropriate permission. If any omissions have been made or if corrections are required, please contact the Publisher.

Cover Design and Art Direction:
Visual Asylum

Cover Illustration
Joel Sotelo

Acknowledgments and credits continue on page 354.

The National Geographic Society
John M. Fahey, Jr., President & Chief Executive Officer
Gilbert M. Grosvenor, Chairman of the Board

National Geographic School Publishing
Hampton-Brown
www.NGSP.com

Printed in the USA
RR Donnelley, Jefferson City, MO

ISBN: 978-0-7362-8009-9

11 12 13 14 15 16 17 18 19

10 9 8 7 6 5 4 3 2

In the U.S.A.™

Unit 1

Nice to Meet You

Unit 2

Your School

Unit 3

Your School Day

Unit 4

Everything You Do

Unit 5

At Lunch

Unit 6

Information Everywhere

Unit 7

How Do You Feel?

Unit 8

Brrr! Put On Your Coat!

Unit 9

Around Town

Unit 10

All Year Long

Unit 1

Nice to Meet You

2

In This Unit

▶ **Language:** Give Personal Information; Make Introductions; Give Information

▶ **Vocabulary:** Greetings and Good-byes; Numbers and Number Words; Family Words; Polite Words; Places

▶ **Reading:** Learn High Frequency Words; Learn Letters and Sounds *Ss, Mm, Ff, Hh, Tt, Aa*; Decode and Spell Words with Short *a*; Retell *From Here to There*

▶ **Writing:** Capitalize Sentences; Capitalize *I*; Use a Period; Write Sentences

Unit Project

CLASS BOOK

1. Write your name and address.

2. Make a list of people in your family.

3. Write where you are from. Collect photos of your home country.

4. Write your information on a class list. Talk about your page.

> My name is Eduardo Vargas.

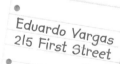

Eduardo Vargas
215 First Street

3

Try Out Language

Listen and Chant

Hello and Good-bye

Hello! My name is Carlos.

Hi! My name is Mai.

See you in class!

See you soon! Good-bye!

Make your own chant. Use your own name.

after school

at lunch

4

Greetings and Good-byes

Listen to each greeting and good-bye.

Say the new words.

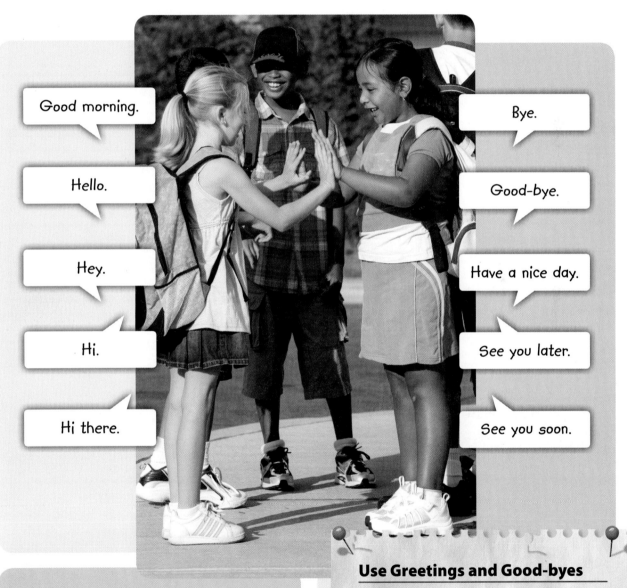

Good morning.

Hello.

Hey.

Hi.

Hi there.

Bye.

Good-bye.

Have a nice day.

See you later.

See you soon.

Use Greetings and Good-byes

Work with a partner. Say hello and good-bye. Then work with a different partner and use different words.

Vocabulary

Numbers and Number Words

👂 Listen to each number. 💬 Say the number words.

0	zero		**11**	eleven
1	one		**12**	twelve
2	two		**13**	thirteen
3	three		**14**	fourteen
4	four		**15**	fifteen
5	five		**16**	sixteen
6	six		**17**	seventeen
7	seven		**18**	eighteen
8	eight		**19**	nineteen
9	nine		**20**	twenty
10	ten			

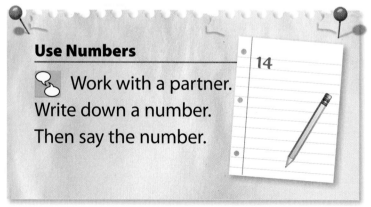

Use Numbers

👥 Work with a partner. Write down a number. Then say the number.

14

6

More Numbers and Number Words

🦻 Listen to each number. 💬 Say the number words.

21	twenty-one
22	twenty-two
23	twenty-three
24	twenty-four
25	twenty-five
26	twenty-six
27	twenty-seven
28	twenty-eight
29	twenty-nine
30	thirty

40	forty
50	fifty
60	sixty
70	seventy
80	eighty
90	ninety
100	one hundred
1,000	one thousand

twenty-two

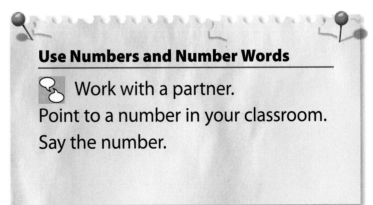

Use Numbers and Number Words

👥 Work with a partner.
Point to a number in your classroom.
Say the number.

Give Personal Information

Listen and Say

Use these sentences to tell about yourself.

My name is _____ .	I live at _____ .	My phone number is _____ .

The School Office

Ms. Estes: Hello.

Denis: Good morning, Ms. Estes. My name is Denis.

Ms. Estes: I need your address and phone number.

Denis: I live at 155 Main Street. My phone number is 520-555-3147.

Ms. Estes: Thank you, Denis.

Denis: Good-bye, Ms. Estes. Have a nice day.

Ms. Estes: Good-bye, Denis. Have a nice day, too.

Student Information Form

Name

Address

Phone Number

Say It Another Way

CD 1 Track 3 ((MP3))

Say addresses and phone numbers in a special way.

	✎ Write It	💬 Say It
Address	155 Main Street	"one fifty-five Main Street"
	5827 Main Street	"fifty-eight twenty-seven Main Street"
Phone Number	520-555-3147	"five two zero – five five five – three one four seven"

Talk Together

Talk to other students. Tell them your name, address, and phone number.

Hi. My name is Jun. I live at 1421 Green Street. My phone number is 713-555-6943.

High Frequency Words

Learn the Alphabet

👂 Listen to your teacher. Point to each letter.

💬 Say the name of each letter.

Aa	Bb	Cc	Dd	Ee	Ff	Gg	Hh	Ii	Jj	Kk	Ll	Mm
Nn	Oo	Pp	Qq	Rr	Ss	Tt	Uu	Vv	Ww	Xx	Yy	Zz

Learn New Words

👂 Listen to your teacher. 💬 Say each new word.

1 **name**
Hi. My name is Mona.

2 **my**
Hello. My name is Pam.

3 **am**
I am a new student.

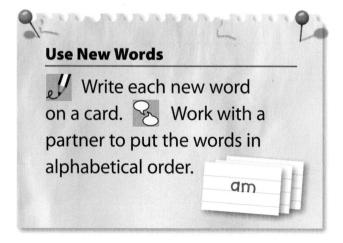

Use New Words

✏️ Write each new word on a card. 🤝 Work with a partner to put the words in alphabetical order.

am

Listen and Say

👂 Listen to your teacher. 💬 Say the name of each picture. Say the first sound.

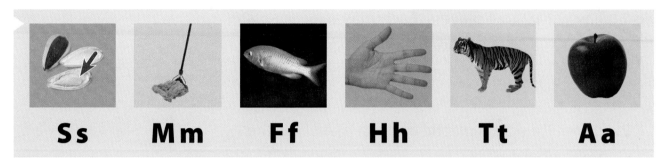

| **S s** | **M m** | **F f** | **H h** | **T t** | **A a** |

👂 Listen to each word. What letter spells the first sound you hear?

Play a Game

How to Play

1. Play with 2 to 4 players. Each player chooses a character on the game board to play.

2. Player 1 places a plastic chip on START on the game board.

3. Player 1 throws a number cube and moves his or her plastic chip the number of spaces on the game board.

4. Player 1 follows the instructions in the space for his or her character.

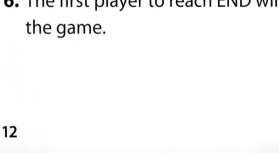

Say your name.

My name is _____.

5. Players take turns.

6. The first player to reach END wins the game.

Rosa Reyes
714 Main Street
830-555-2587

Mark Jones
41 Oak Street
702-555-6340

Go ahead one space.

Say your name.

Say good-bye to someone.

Say hello to someone.

END

Say where you live.

Say your phone number.

Go back one space.

Say hello to someone.

Say where you live.

Say good-bye to someone.

Go ahead one space.

Say your name.

Say where you live.

Say good-bye to someone.

Say hello to someone.

Say your phone number.

Got Your Name!
Got Your Number!

Go back to START.

START

Say hello to someone.

Say your phone number.

Go back one space.

Say where you live.

Go ahead one space.

Say your name.

Saba Ali
222 Elm Street
747-555-4017

Joe Thompson
1925 Third Street
520-555-3194

13

This Is My Family

This is my father,
And this is my mother.
This is my sister,
And this is my brother.

We are glad to meet you.
We hope you feel the same.
Please stay and talk to us.
Let's learn each other's names.

Family Words

Look at the pictures in the family tree.

Listen to your teacher.

Say the word for each family member.

1
my grandfather

2
my grandmother

3
my grandfather

4
my grandmother

5
my aunt

6
my uncle

7
my father

8
my mother

9
my cousin

10
my brother

11
my sister

12 me

Polite Words

Listen to your teacher.

> Use the word **please** when you want someone
> to do something.

Please sit down.

Please take one.

> To thank someone, say **thank you**.
> If someone thanks you, say **you're welcome**.

Thank you.

You're welcome.

Say the polite words for the pictures.

1 Please come in.

2 Thank you.

You're welcome.

3 Please open this.

Use Polite Words

Look at the pictures again. Work with a partner. What other polite words can you add? Act them out.

Make Introductions

Listen and Say

Use words and sentences like these when you introduce or meet people.

INTRODUCTION	RESPONSES		
_____ , this is _____ .	Hello, _____ . Hi, _____ .	Nice to meet you.	Glad to meet you, too.

This Is Katie

Maya: Amy, this is Katie.
Katie, this is my friend Amy.

Amy: Hi, Katie. Nice to meet you.

Katie: Glad to meet you, too.

HELLO
Peter

Say It Another Way

People use different ways to make introductions.

Ways to Introduce People	Ways to Respond	More Things to Say
This is Katie. I want you to meet Katie. I would like you to meet Katie.	Nice to meet you. Glad to meet you. It's a pleasure to meet you.	How are you? / I'm fine. Thank you.

Talk Together

 Work with two partners. Act out the scene.

High Frequency Words

Learn About Words

👂 Listen to your teacher. Point to each letter. Start with **S**.

💬 Say a letter. Say the word.

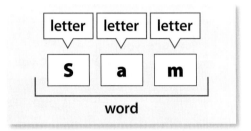

letter | letter | letter
S | **a** | **m**

word

Learn New Words

👂 Listen to your teacher.

💬 Say each new word.

1 **I**

| **I** | live at 24 Main Street.

2 **is**

My home **is** at 24 Main Street.

3 **you**

You live on my street.

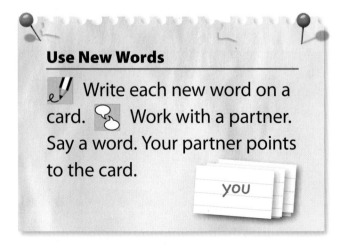

Use New Words

✏️ Write each new word on a card. ✋ Work with a partner. Say a word. Your partner points to the card.

you

20

a

Read a Word

Blend the sounds to read a word.

Read More Words

Read the words to a partner.

1 am
2 ham
3 Sam
4 at
5 cat

6 fat
7 hat
8 mat
9 sat

h
ha
hat

Make New Words

Use these letters. Write words on cards. Practice reading with a partner.

s m f

h t a

mat

CD 1
Track 7   (((MP3)))

Theme Theater

Yuen and his family are having a party. His good friend
Eric is there. Listen to the conversation. Then act it out.

What Do I Say?

YUEN: My Aunt Ying is coming to the party.
I will meet her today.
What will I say to her?

CHORUS: *Yuen will meet his aunt today.*
What will he say?
What will he say?

ERIC: Say hello to her.
Say you are glad to see her.

YUEN: Then what do I say?

ERIC: Then introduce yourself.

◇   ◇   ◇

[Aunt Ying arrives.]

CHORUS: *What will Yuen say?*
Do you know?
Eric tells Yuen to say hello.

YUEN: Hello, Aunt Ying. Please come in.
My name is Yuen.

AUNT YING: Hello, nephew. I am glad to
see you. You are so tall!

YUEN: Aunt Ying, this is my friend Eric.
Eric, this is my aunt, Aunt Ying.

ERIC: Hello, Aunt Ying. Nice to meet you.

AUNT YING: Hi, Eric. Glad to meet you, too!

ERIC: I have my camera. May I please take your picture?

YUEN: Yes! Thank you!

CHORUS: *Eric is a very good friend.*
He takes a picture of Aunt Ying and Yuen.

Let's Be Friends

I am **Pablo**. I'm from **Cuba**.

I live in **Flagstaff, Arizona**.

I'd like to meet you and get to know you.

We **Cubans** are a friendly bunch if I may show you.

I am **Tanya**. I'm from **Russia**.

I live in **Stockton**, **California**.

Yes, I've heard that you are friendly

From Mei Ling, Marta, Mariluz, and my friend Kim-Ly!

Make your own song with a partner. Use your own name, home country, and place where you live.

The United States of America

 Listen to your teacher. 🗨 Say the name of each state.

★ = capital of the United States

Name the States

🗨 Work with a partner. Point to a state on the map. Say the name of that state.

Places in the World

Listen to the places in the world.

Say the names.

Haiti

Mexico

Cuba

Guatemala

Sabrina

El Salvador

Jamaica

Colombia

Dominican Republic

Peru

Oscar

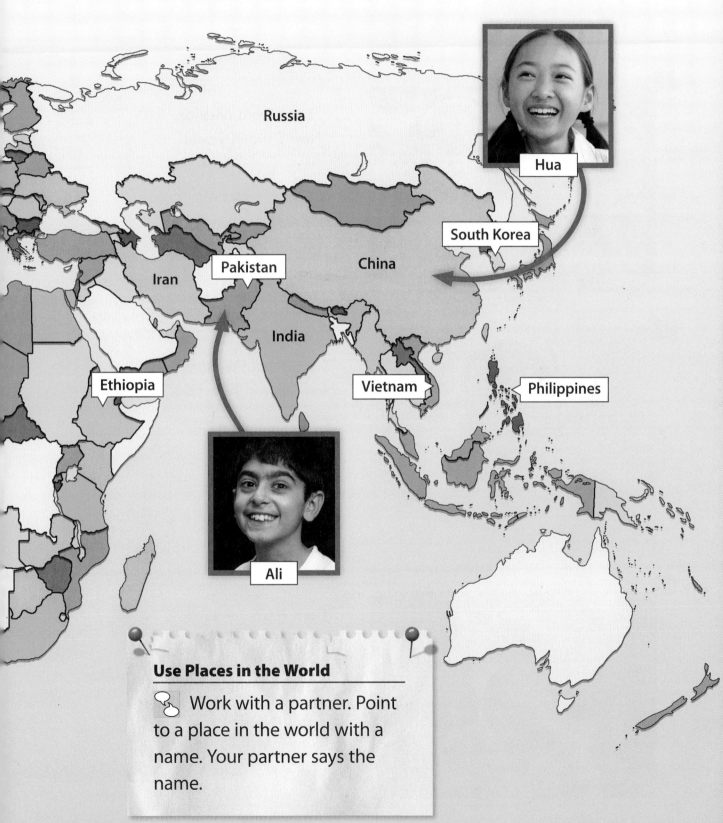

Russia

Hua

South Korea

China

Pakistan

Iran

India

Ethiopia

Vietnam

Philippines

Ali

Use Places in the World

Work with a partner. Point to a place in the world with a name. Your partner says the name.

27

Give Information

Listen and Say

Use these sentences to talk about yourself.

| I am from _____ . | Now I live in _____ . |

1

"I am from Mexico.
Now I live in Texas."

2

"I am from Pakistan.
Now I live in New York."

3

"I am from Jamaica.
Now I live in California."

Say It Another Way

When you talk about yourself, use **I am** or **I'm**.

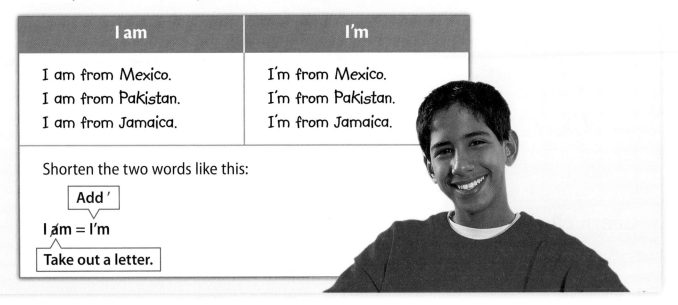

I am	I'm
I am from Mexico.	I'm from Mexico.
I am from Pakistan.	I'm from Pakistan.
I am from Jamaica.	I'm from Jamaica.

Shorten the two words like this:

Add '

I am = I'm

Take out a letter.

Talk Together

Work with a partner. Show a picture of your country.
Introduce yourself.

Word File Pictures
🔵 NGReach.com

Hi. My name is Irina.
I am from Russia.
Now I live in New York.
I live at 456 Maple Street.

Russia

High Frequency Words

Learn About Sentences

🦻 Listen to your teacher. Point to each word. Start with **My**.

💬 Say a word. Say the sentence.

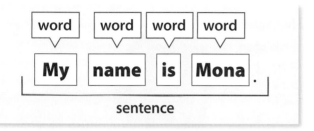

word | word | word | word

My | **name** | **is** | **Mona** .

sentence

Learn New Words

🦻 Listen to your teacher. 💬 Say each new word.

1 **me**
My father gave this to **me** .

2 **show**
Show me your family.

3 **look**
You can **look** at them here.

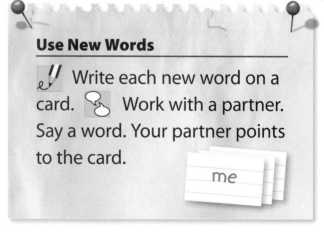

Use New Words

✏️ Write each new word on a card. 🖐️ Work with a partner. Say a word. Your partner points to the card.

me

Letters and Sounds

Spell and Read

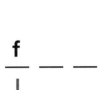 Look at the picture. Use your letter cards to spell the word.

Then read the word.

| a | t |

| a | m |

1

f __ __

2

m __ __

3

h __ __

4

T __ __

5

h __ __

Sam
S-a-m
Sam

Spell More Words

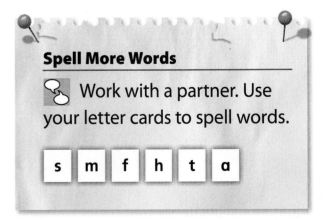 Work with a partner. Use your letter cards to spell words.

| s | m | f | h | t | a |

Listen and Read Along

 Think about who is in the story.

From Here to There

by Margery Cuyler

illustrated by Yu Cha Pak

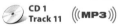
CD 1
Track 11 (((MP3)))

Maria Mendoza

Maria's father

Maria's mother
and brother

Maria's sister

Talk About It

1 Who is the story about?

2 Where does she live?

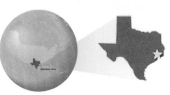

Splendora, Texas U.S.A.

Reread and Retell

3 Make a circle diagram to show where Maria lives. Notice that her home is in the smallest circle.

4 Now use your completed diagram as you tell a partner about Maria.

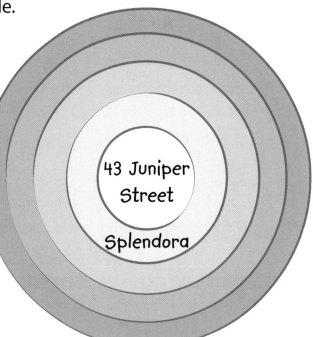

43 Juniper Street

Splendora

Write About Yourself

Learn About Sentences

Some sentences tell something.
They end with a period.

I am from Mexico. $\triangleleft$ period

Start every sentence with a capital letter.
Always capitalize the word **I**.

Now **I** live in Chicago, Illinois.
^   ^
capital letters

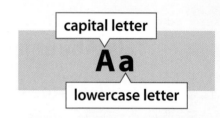

capital letter

Aa

lowercase letter

Letters	
Aa	Nn
Bb	Oo
Cc	Pp
Dd	Qq
Ee	Rr
Ff	Ss
Gg	Tt
Hh	Uu
Ii	Vv
Jj	Ww
Kk	Xx
Ll	Yy
Mm	Zz

Copy each sentence. Use capital letters and periods.

1. now i live here

2. i live with my family

3. my phone number is 828-555-2323

4. i live at 19 Main Street

5. my aunt and uncle live here, too

6. my grandparents live in Mexico

Study a Model

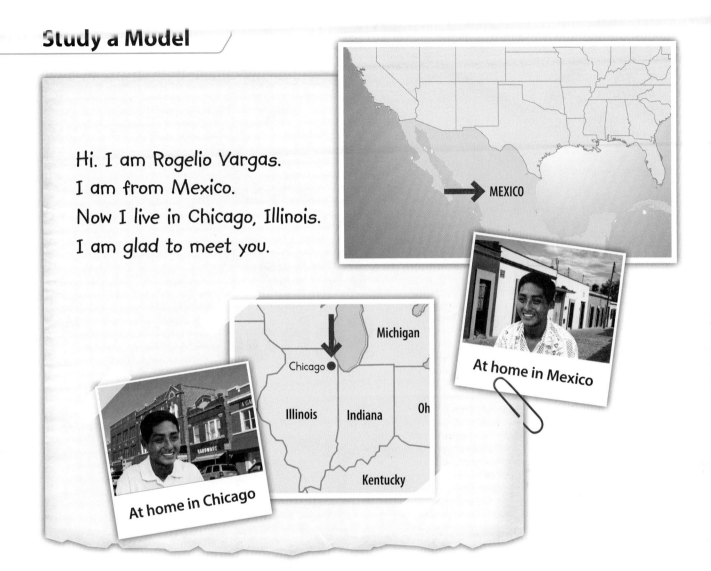

Hi. I am Rogelio Vargas.
I am from Mexico.
Now I live in Chicago, Illinois.
I am glad to meet you.

MEXICO

At home in Mexico

Michigan

Chicago

Illinois   Indiana   Oh

Kentucky

At home in Chicago

Write

Now write about yourself. Create your own class yearbook page. Draw pictures or tape photos of yourself to your page.

Check Your Writing

Read your work to a partner. Check the writing.
Do you need to add a period to the end of a sentence?
Do you need to add any capital letters?

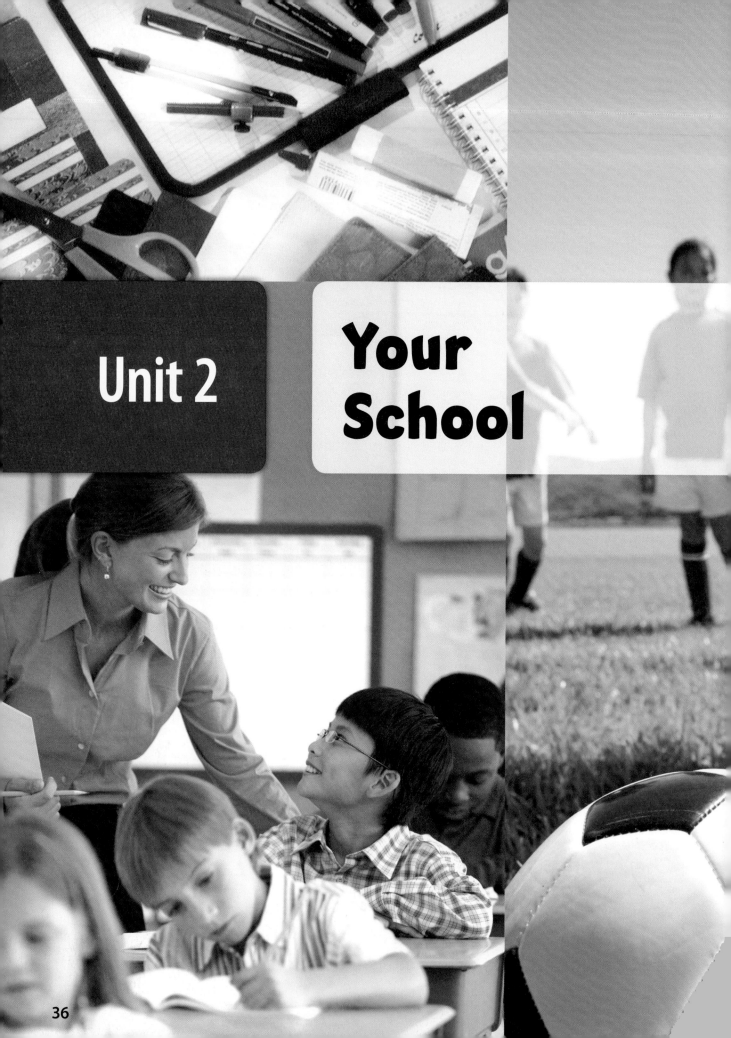

Unit 2

Your School

In This Unit

▶ **Language:** Give Information; Ask and Answer Questions; Give and Follow Commands

▶ **Vocabulary:** School Tools; Colors and Sizes; Classroom Objects; Shapes; School Places and Things

▶ **Reading:** Learn High Frequency Words; Read Decodable Text; Summarize *Shapes*

▶ **Writing:** Capitalize Sentences; Capitalize Names of Countries, Cities, and States; Write Sentences

Unit Project

OLD SCHOOL SCRAPBOOK

1 Think about your home country. List what you remember.

2 Gather pictures and things from your old home and school.

3 Show things from your school. Tell about your school.

This is the board.

Try Out Language

Listen and Chant

CoolTools

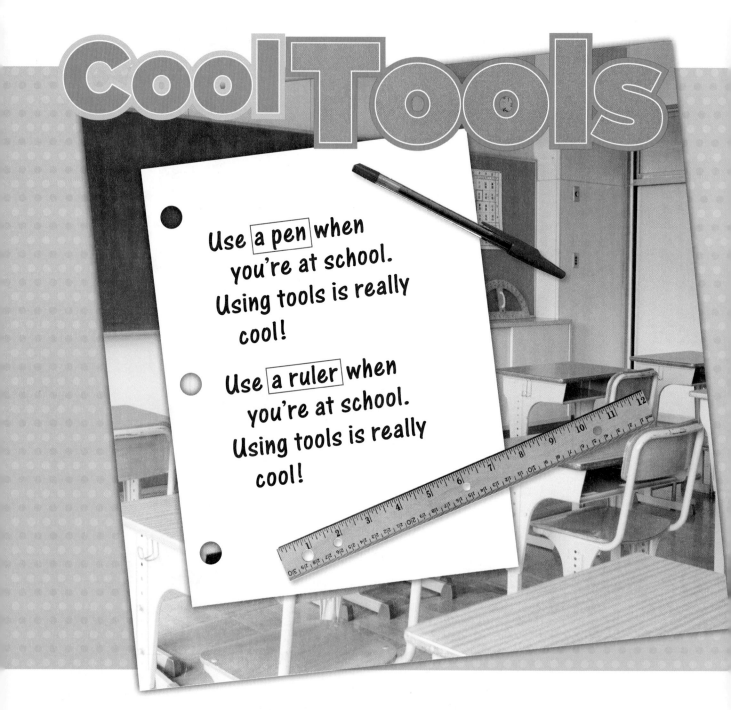

Use a pen when you're at school. Using tools is really cool!

Use a ruler when you're at school. Using tools is really cool!

Make your own chant.

a stapler

a book

a calculator

a notebook

a pencil

Colors and Sizes

Listen to your teacher.

Use these words for colors and sizes.

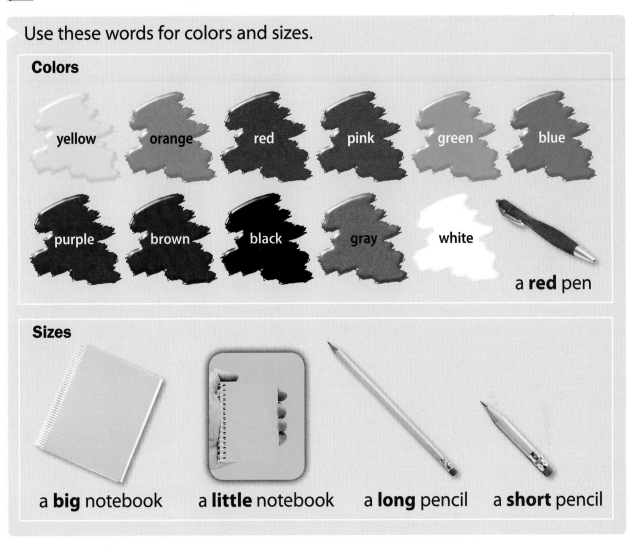

Colors

yellow   orange   red   pink   green   blue

purple   brown   black   gray   white

a **red** pen

Sizes

a **big** notebook   a **little** notebook   a **long** pencil   a **short** pencil

Listen to your teacher.   Say the words.

1   a long pencil

2   a short ruler

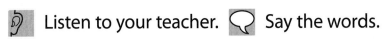

3   a green notebook

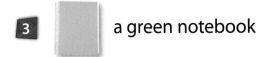

4   a blue pair of scissors

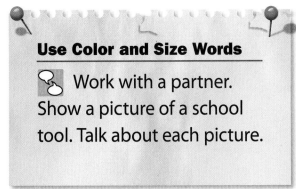

Use Color and Size Words

Work with a partner.
Show a picture of a school
tool. Talk about each picture.

School Tools, Colors, and Sizes

🎧 Listen to your teacher.

💬 Say the name of each tool and its color or size.

KEY WORDS

a book	black	big
a calculator	blue	little
an eraser	brown	long
a notebook	green	short
a pair of scissors	orange	
a pen	pink	
a pencil	purple	
a piece of paper	red	
a ruler	white	
a stapler	yellow	

COOL SHAPES

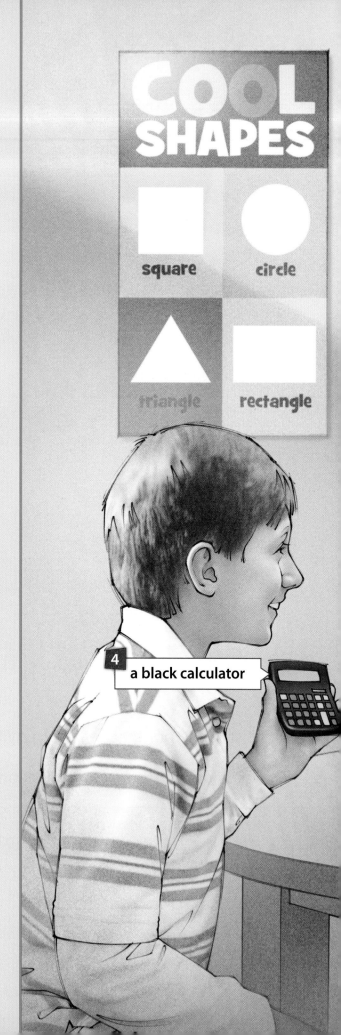

square   circle

triangle   rectangle

1

a little eraser

2

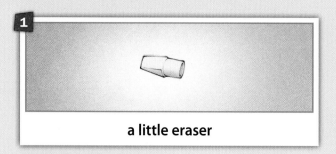

a short, red ruler

3

a black stapler

4   a black calculator

Listen and Say

Use sentences like these to tell about things in your classroom.

| This is _____ . | Here is _____ . | I have _____ . |
| It is _____ . | It is _____ . | It is _____ . |

1

"This is a ruler.
It is long."

2

"Here is an eraser.
It is green."

3

"I have a notebook.
It is big."

Use the Right Word

a	an
Use **a** if the next word starts with a consonant sound. **a** book **a** notebook **a** pencil	Use **an** if the next word starts with a vowel sound. **an** eraser
Consonants: b, c, d, f, g, h, j, k, l, m, n, p, q, r, s, t, v, w, x, y, z	**Vowels:** a, e, i, o, u

Talk Together

Work with a partner. Talk about the tools you use in school. Tell about their colors and sizes.

This is a notebook. It is green. It is big.

Ask and Answer Questions

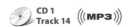
Listen and Say

Use questions like these to find out the names of things.

Is this _____ ?	Is this _____ ?	Is this _____ ?
Yes, it is.	No, it is not.	No, it is not. It's _____ .
	No, it isn't.	No, it isn't. It's _____ .

1

"Is this a pen?"      "Yes, it is."

2

"Is this a pen?"   "No, it is not."

3

"Is this a stapler?"   "No, it isn't. It's a ruler."

44

How It Works

Ask a question to get information.

A question starts with a **capital letter** and ends with a **question mark**.

capital letter

"Is this a pen**?**"

question mark

Answer questions like these with **yes** or **no**.

Talk Together

Work with a partner. Ask questions about the tools you use in school. Answer the questions with *Yes, it is* or *No, it isn't. It's _____* .

Is this a ruler?

No, it isn't. It's a stapler.

High Frequency Words

Review

💬 Read each word aloud. Use the correct word in each sentence.

me	my

Is	Show

I	Look

1 Show ＿＿＿＿＿＿＿ a pen.

2 ＿＿＿＿＿＿＿ me a pencil.

3 ＿＿＿＿＿＿＿ at this book.

Learn New Words

👂 Listen to your teacher.

💬 Say each new word.

4 **point**
Please **point** to your book.

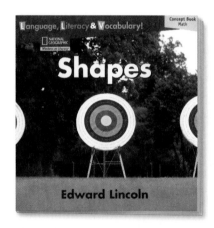

Language, Literacy & Vocabulary!

Concept Book Math

NATIONAL GEOGRAPHIC

Shapes

Edward Lincoln

5 **this**
This is my book.

6 **the**
The book is very nice.

Use New Words

💬 Say a sentence with a blank for a new word. Your partner says the sentence with the new word.

＿＿＿ is my book.

This is my book.

Listen and Chant

 Listen to the chant.   Say the chant with your teacher.

My Name Is Sam

Sam, Sam.
My name is Sam.

Matt, Matt.
My name is Matt.

I am Sam.

I am Matt.

Sam sat.

Matt sat.

Matt sat. Matt!

Use Letters and Sounds

How many sounds does each
word have? Tell a partner.

Sam   Matt   sat

Wrap-Up

Play a Game

How to Play

1. Play with a partner.

1

2

2. Make a spinner with a paper clip. Hold it in the center of the circle with a pencil.

3. Partner 1 spins and asks a question.

Is this a pencil?

Is this an eraser?

4. Partner 2 answers.

Yes, it is.

No, it isn't. It's _____ .

5. Then Partner 2 spins.

What Is It?

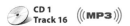

CD 1
Track 16   ((MP3))

Listen and Chant

In the Classroom

Here is a [desk]. Here is a chair.

Here are students everywhere.

Make your own chant.

bookcase   table   map   clock

Shapes

Listen to your teacher.

Here are the names of four shapes.

circle

triangle

rectangle

square

Listen to your teacher. Say each sentence.

1 The piece of paper is a rectangle.

2 The clock is a circle.

3 The table is a square.

4 The map is a rectangle.

5 The ruler is a triangle.

6 The bookcase is a rectangle.

7 The piece of paper is a triangle.

Name More Shapes

Work with a partner. Find things in your classroom for each shape.
Draw a picture on a card. Your partner names the shape.

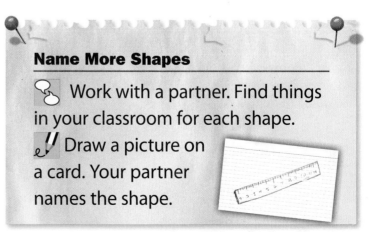

In the Classroom

Look at each picture.

Listen to your teacher.

Say the name of the item.

1 map

2 computer

3 clock

4 student

5

table

6

chair

7

bookcase

8 board

READ CHAPTERS 4 & 5.
ANSWER THE QUESTIONS
AT THE END OF EACH CHAPTER.

9 teacher

10 desk

Guess the Object

🗣 Work with a partner. Find things with different shapes in your classroom. Tell the color, size, and shape. Your partner names the thing.

It is big. It is brown. It is a rectangle.

A table!

Give and Follow Commands

Listen and Say

Use words like these to give a command.

| Show me _____ . | Point to _____ . |

1 Show me a pen.

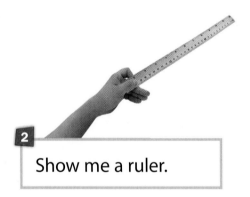

2 Show me a ruler.

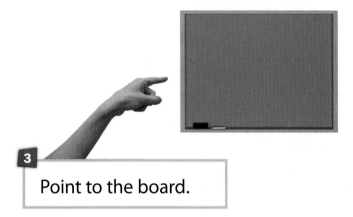

3 Point to the board.

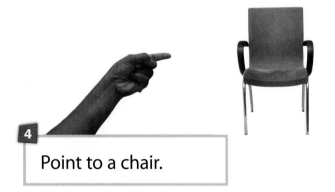

4 Point to a chair.

54

Use the Right Word

a	the
Use **a** to talk about one thing that is not specific.	Use **the** to talk about a specific thing.
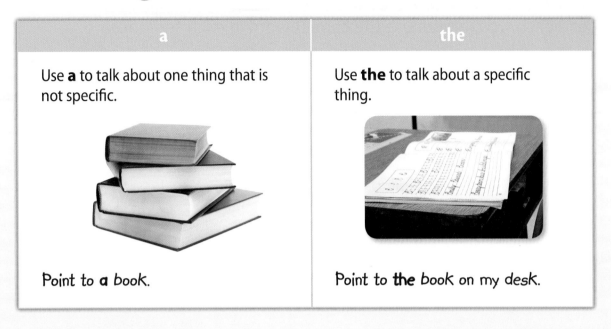	
Point to **a** book.	Point to **the** book on my desk.

Talk Together

Take turns with a partner. Give commands and follow commands. Use things in the classroom.

Show me a notebook.

High Frequency Words

Review

🗨 Read each word aloud. Use the correct word in each sentence.

this	**the**

my	**am**

I	**you**

1 Ann, _____ is Pat.

2 Pat is _____ brother.

3 Glad to meet _____ .

Learn New Words

👂 Listen to your teacher.   🗨 Say each new word.

4 **school**
Is this my new **school** ?

5 **yes**
Yes , this is your new school.

6 **it**
It is a big school.

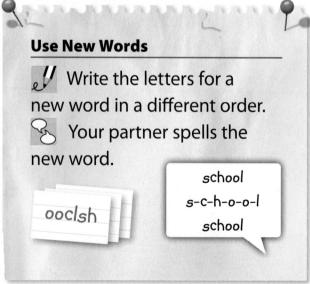

Use New Words

✏ Write the letters for a new word in a different order.
🖐 Your partner spells the new word.

ooclsh

school
s-c-h-o-o-l
school

I AM MATT

CD 1
Track 18 MP3

Theme Theater

Today is Miguel and Gloria's first day of school. Listen to their conversation. Then act it out.

The First Day of School

MIGUEL: This is our new classroom.
Look at that map, Gloria!

GLORIA: It is big!

MRS. JONES: Hello, students. I am Mrs. Jones.
I am your new teacher.

MIGUEL: Hi. My name is Miguel.

GLORIA: Hello. My name is Gloria.

MIGUEL: Can you show us the classoom, please?

MRS. JONES: Yes. Here are your desks and chairs. Here is a bookcase.

GLORIA: Do you have a computer?

MRS. JONES: Yes. Here is the computer. Everyone shares it.

CHORUS: *Here is a desk. Here is a chair.*
Here is the computer
for students to share.

◊   ◊   ◊

MRS. JONES: Do you have everything you need for the class?

MIGUEL: I think so. I have a pen, a pencil, and a notebook.

GLORIA: I do, too. I also have a ruler and a calculator.

CHORUS: *Miguel has a pen, a pencil,*
and a notebook.
Gloria has a ruler and
a calculator.

MRS. JONES: Hello, everyone. Please sit down.

Listen and Sing

CD 1
Track 19
((MP3))

WHAT'S IN OUR SCHOOL?

What's in our school?
What's in our school?
Do you know what is in our school?

Look over there.
I see a gym.
A gym is in our school.

Make your own song.

gym

window

classroom

map

Vocabulary

School Places

🦻 Listen to your teacher.

🗨 Say the name of each place or thing.

KEY WORDS

door	flagpole
entrance	main building
fence	steps
field	track
flag	window

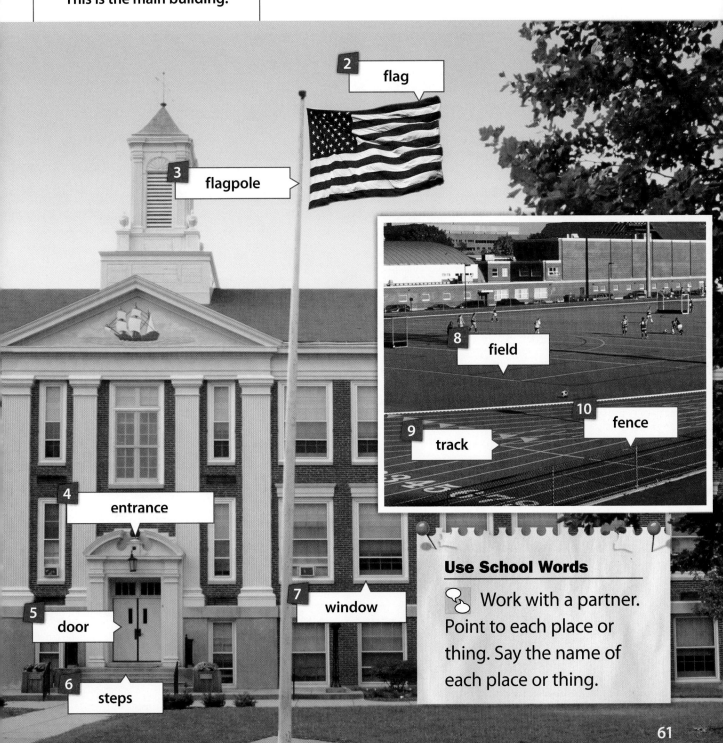

1 This is the main building.

2 flag

3 flagpole

8 field

10 fence

9 track

4 entrance

5 door

7 window

6 steps

Use School Words

🗨 Work with a partner. Point to each place or thing. Say the name of each place or thing.

Vocabulary

School Places and Things

👂 Listen to your teacher.

💬 Say the name of each place or thing.

KEY WORDS

bathroom	money	soap
cafeteria	napkin	spoon
fork	paper towel	toilet
knife	plate	tray
line	sink	water

1 This is the cafeteria.

2 line

3 tray

4 money

5 fork

6 spoon

7 knife

8 napkin

9 plate

62

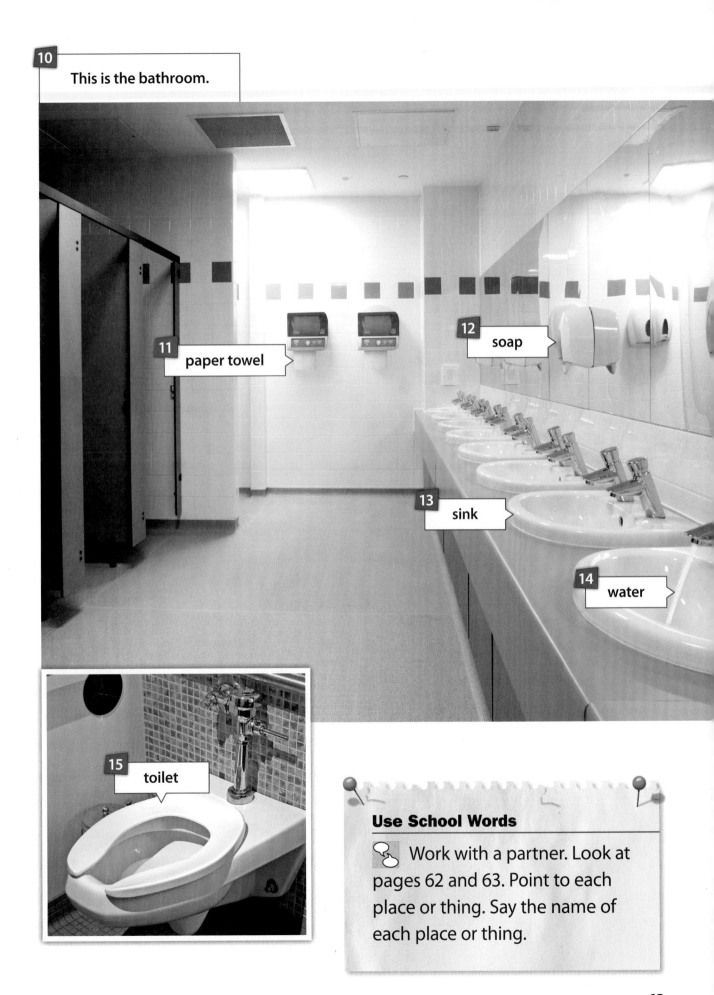

10 This is the bathroom.

11 paper towel

12 soap

13 sink

14 water

15 toilet

Use School Words

Work with a partner. Look at pages 62 and 63. Point to each place or thing. Say the name of each place or thing.

63

Ask and Answer Questions

Listen and Say

Use sentences like these to talk about where things are.

QUESTIONS	ANSWERS
What is in the _____?	A _____ is in the _____.
What is on the _____?	A _____ is on the _____.

1

"What is in the classroom?"

"A desk is in the classroom."

2

"What is on the desk?"

"A book is on the desk."

Use the Right Word

Use **in** and **on** to tell where things are.

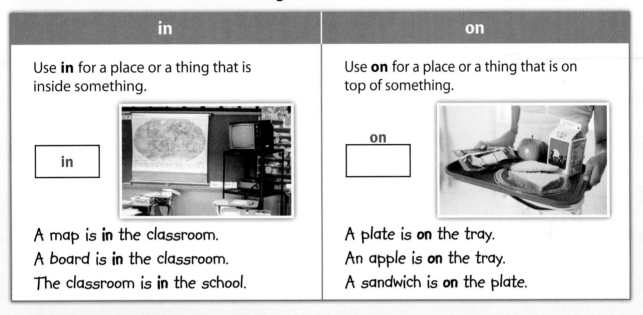

in	on
Use **in** for a place or a thing that is inside something.	Use **on** for a place or a thing that is on top of something.
in	on
A map is **in** the classroom.	A plate is **on** the tray.
A board is **in** the classroom.	An apple is **on** the tray.
The classroom is **in** the school.	A sandwich is **on** the plate.

Talk Together

Work with a partner. Look around your classroom.
Ask and answer questions with *in* or *on*.

What is on the table?

A computer is on the table.

High Frequency Words

Review

💬 Read each word aloud. Use the correct word in each sentence.

school	show

1 Is this your _____ ?

You	Yes

2 _____ , it is my school.

it	is

3 It _____ big.

Learn New Words

👂 Listen to your teacher.   💬 Say each new word.

4 **number**
Is this room number 3?

5 **no**
No , it is not.

6 **not**
It is not your classroom.

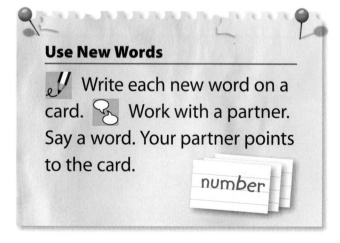

Use New Words

✍️ Write each new word on a card. 🤝 Work with a partner. Say a word. Your partner points to the card.

number

66

FAT SAM

I am Matt.

This is Sam.

SAM IS FAT.

SAM LOOKS AT THE HAM.

NO!

Look at Sam!

SAM HAS MY HAT!

Listen and Read Along

 Think about the book. What is it about?

Language, Literacy & Vocabulary!

Concept Book
Math

NATIONAL GEOGRAPHIC
Windows on Literacy

Shapes

Edward Lincoln

CD 1
Track 21   (((MP3)))

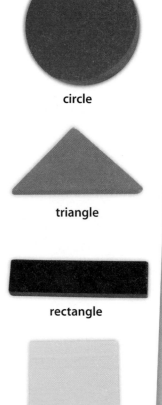

circle

triangle

rectangle

square

clock

present

Talk About It

1 What is the book about?

2 What kinds of shapes does the book tell about?

sign

paper

Reread and Retell

3 Make a concept map to tell about different shapes. Use each section to tell about one shape.

4 Now use your completed concept map as you tell a partner about shapes.

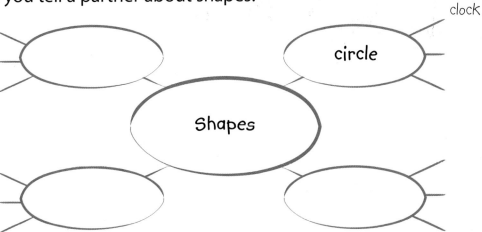

clock

circle

Shapes

Write About Your Schools

Learn About Capital Letters

Remember to start every sentence with a **capital letter**.

Here is my school.

capital letter

Start the names of cities, states, and countries with a capital letter, too.

capital letters

I am from Monterrey, Mexico.
Now I live in Dallas, Texas.

Copy each sentence. Use capital letters.

1. this is my school.

2. i live in miami, florida.

3. i am from vietnam.

4. i live in chicago, illinois.

5. i am from russia.

6. my sister and brother are here, too.

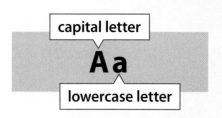

| capital letter |
| Aa |
| lowercase letter |

Letters	
Aa	Nn
Bb	Oo
Cc	Pp
Dd	Qq
Ee	Rr
Ff	Ss
Gg	Tt
Hh	Uu
Ii	Vv
Jj	Ww
Kk	Xx
Ll	Yy
Mm	Zz

Study a Model

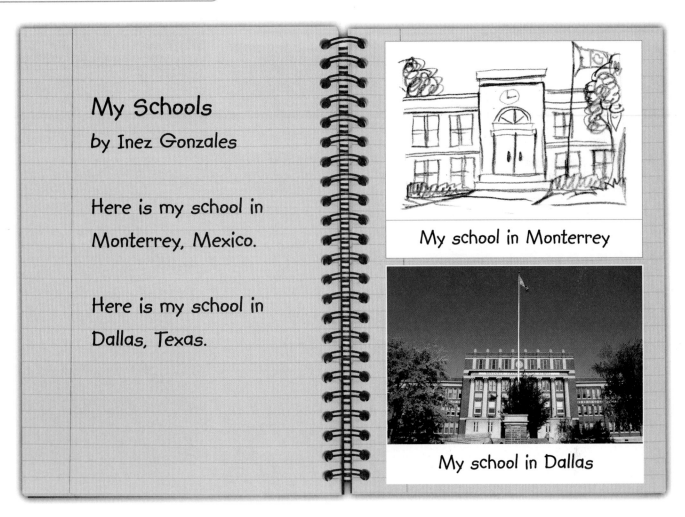

My Schools
by Inez Gonzales

Here is my school in
Monterrey, Mexico.

Here is my school in
Dallas, Texas.

My school in Monterrey

My school in Dallas

Write

Now write about your old school and your new school. Create your own journal page. Draw pictures or tape photos of your schools to your page.

Check Your Writing

Read your work to a partner. Check the writing.
Use a capital letter for the first word of a sentence.
Use capital letters for the names of cities, states, or countries.

Unit 3

Your School Day

In This Unit

▶ **Language:** Ask and Answer Questions

▶ **Vocabulary:** Time and Days of the Week; School Subjects; School Places and Workers

▶ **Reading:** Learn High Frequency Words; Learn Letters and Sounds *Nn, Ll, Pp, Gg, Ii*; Decode and Spell words with Short *i*; Summarize *Time and Routines*

▶ **Writing:** Capitalize *I*; Capitalize Names of Cities, Streets, People, and Days of the Week; Write Sentences

Unit Project

NEW SCHOOL DIRECTORY

1 Who do you see at school? Draw or take pictures of people. Make a page for each person.

2 Put your pages in order. Make a book.

3 Read your book aloud. Tell about your day.

> Mr. Gomez is the librarian. He is in the library.

Mr. Gomez

73

Listen and Chant

WHAT TIME IS IT?

What time is it?
What time is it?

It's one o'clock
in the afternoon.

I have to meet my
friend in class.

Oh, that's
very soon!

Make your own chant.

twelve thirty

two o'clock

three o'clock

74

Times and Days of the Week

 Listen to your teacher. Say the words for times and days.

Times of Day

| morning | noon | afternoon | evening | night |

Days of the Week

Sunday   Monday   Tuesday   Wednesday   Thursday   Friday   Saturday

 Listen to your teacher. Say the day and time of day.

1

It's Monday morning.

3

It's Sunday afternoon.

2

It's Tuesday evening.

Tell the Day and Time

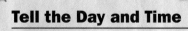 Tell a partner the day and time of day in each picture.

Vocabulary

Telling Time

Listen to your teacher.

Use numbers or words to tell the time.

Write:	9:00	10:15	11:30	12:00	12:45	1:10	2:40
Say:	nine o'clock	ten fifteen	eleven thirty	twelve o'clock	twelve forty-five	one ten	two forty
Or say:		a quarter past ten	half past eleven	noon (or midnight)	a quarter to one	ten after one	twenty to three

Listen to your teacher. Say the time on each clock.

1

8:00

3

7:15

5

8:10

2

5:40

4

12:00

Tell Time

Tell a partner the time in each picture.

eight o'clock

What Time Is It? What Day Is It?

🦻 Listen to your teacher. 💬 Say the time, day, and time of day.

1

12:00

Sunday noon

2

6:10

Monday evening

3

6:45

Tuesday morning

4

3:00

Wednesday afternoon

5

Thursday morning

6

Friday night

7

Saturday afternoon

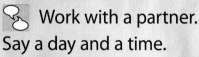

Tell a Day and Time

🖐 Work with a partner. Say a day and a time.
✏️ Your partner draws a picture of what he or she does then.

77

Ask and Answer Questions

 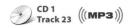
Listen and Say

Use questions like these to find out the time and the day.

QUESTION	ANSWERS	
What time is it?	It is _____ .	It's _____ .
What day is it?	It is _____ .	It's _____ .

1 What time is it?   It is 10:00.

3 What day is it?   It is Monday.

2 What time is it?   It's 5:30.

4 What day is it?   It's Friday.

78

Say It Another Way

CD 1 Track 24 ((MP3))

People use different ways to ask for the time.

Ask for the Time	Tell the Time
What's the time?	It's six ten.
Do you have the time?	Yes, it's six ten.
What time do you have?	I have six ten.
Can you please tell me the time?	Yes, my watch says six ten.

Talk Together

Write a day and draw a time on a card. Show your card to others. Ask questions about the day and the time.

What day is it?
What time is it?

Tuesday

High Frequency Words

Review

💬 Read each word aloud. Use the correct word in each sentence.

number	name

school	not

Yes	No

1 I am in room _____ 5.

2 It is _____ big.

3 _____ , it is not.

Learn New Words

👂 Listen to your teacher. 💬 Say each new word.

4 **time**
What **time** is it?

5 **at**
It's 11:30. Lunch is **at** noon.

6 **day**
I bring my lunch every **day** .

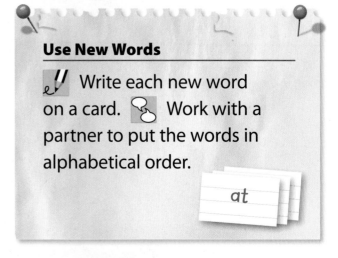

Use New Words

✍️ Write each new word on a card. 🐾 Work with a partner to put the words in alphabetical order.

at

Letters and Sounds

Listen and Say

👂 Listen to your teacher. 💬 Say the name of each picture. Say the first sound.

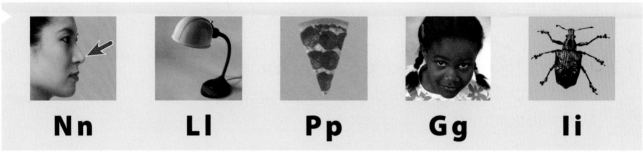

| Nn | Ll | Pp | Gg | Ii |

👂 Listen to each word. What letter spells the first sound you hear?

1
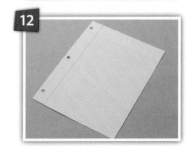

2
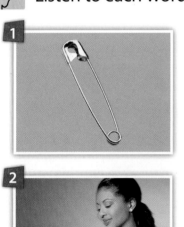

3

4

5

6

7
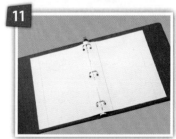

8

9
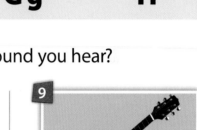

10
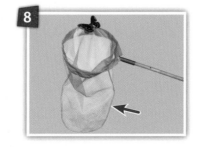

11

12

Play a Game

How to Play

1. Play with a partner.

2. Partner 1 tosses a plastic chip onto the game board to make it land on a day. Then Partner 1 asks about the day.

Thursday

What day is it?

3. Partner 2 answers.

It is Thursday.

4. Partner 1 tosses a plastic chip onto the game board to make it land on a time. Partner 1 asks about the time.

What time is it?

5. Partner 2 answers.

It's two thirty.

6. Partners take turns.

What Day Is It?

Sunday	Monday	Tuesday	Wednesday	Thursday	Friday	Saturday

What Time Is It?

Listen and Sing

My Schedule

I am going to science class soon.

I am going to science class soon.

When I'm done with science class,

It's time for social studies class.

Then I will eat my lunch around noon.

Make your own song.

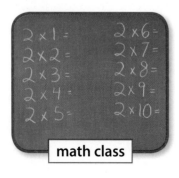

2 x 1 =   2 x 6 =
2 x 2 =   2 x 7 =
2 x 3 =   2 x 8 =
2 x 4 =   2 x 9 =
2 x 5 =   2 x 10 =

math class

P.E. class

Hi. My name is Juan.

ESL class

School Subjects

👓 Look at each picture.

👂 Listen to your teacher.

🗨 Say the name of each school subject.

KEY WORDS

ESL class	math class
homeroom	P.E.
language arts class	science class
lunch	social studies class

1

ESL class

4

lunch

7

science class

2

homeroom

5

math class

8

social studies class

3

language arts class

6

P.E.

Use School Words

 Work with a partner. Point to a picture. Your partner says the name of the class.

85

Ask and Answer Questions

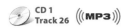
Listen and Say

Use questions like these to find out the time and place of your classes.

QUESTION	ANSWERS
When is _____ ?	It's at _____ .
Where is _____ ?	It's in _____ .

Use the Right Word

Use **at** and **in** to talk about times and places.

	at	in
Times	**at** 10:00 **at** lunch **at** night	**in** the morning **in** the afternoon **in** the evening
Places	**at** school **at** home	**in** the gym **in** Room 105

Talk Together

Work with a partner. Ask questions about your partner's school day. Your partner answers.

When is P.E. class?

It's at 10 o'clock.

High Frequency Words

Review

 Read each word aloud. Use the correct word in each sentence.

show	school

Yes	You

not	no

 1 Do you like _____ ?

2 _____ , I do.

3 But I do _____ like the food.

Learn New Words

Listen to your teacher.   Say each new word.

4 **what**
  What do you have for lunch today?

5 **tomorrow**
  I have a sandwich.
  Tomorrow I will have a taco.

6 **who**
  Who makes your lunch?

Use New Words

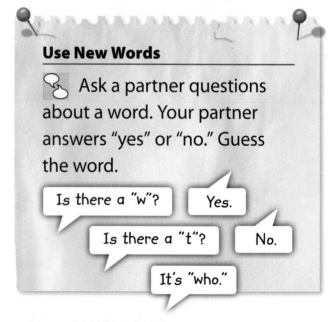 Ask a partner questions about a word. Your partner answers "yes" or "no." Guess the word.

Is there a "w"?   Yes.

Is there a "t"?   No.

It's "who."

88

Letters and Sounds

Read a Word

💬 Blend the sounds to read a word.

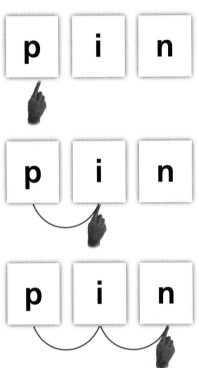

| p | i | n |

| p | i | n |

| p | i | n |

p
pi
pin

Read More Words

💬 Read the words to a partner.

1	it		6	in
2	hit		7	pin
3	sit		8	fin
4	pit		9	tin
5	pig			

Make New Words

✏️ Use these letters. Write words on cards. 🖐 Practice reading with a partner.

n	p	g	h
s	t	i	

pig

Theme Theater

Monique is studying for a science test. She is talking to her brother. Listen to their conversation. Then act it out.

Up Too Late

ALFRED: What are you doing, Monique? It's ten o'clock at night.

MONIQUE: I am studying. I have a science test on Wednesday.

CHORUS: *Monique has a test in science class. She is studying.*

◊   ◊   ◊

[It is the next morning.]

ALFRED: Monique! Wake up!

MONIQUE: *[confused]* What? What time is it?

ALFRED: It's seven thirty in the morning.

MONIQUE: I'm tired. I studied all night.

ALFRED: Get ready for school now!

CHORUS: *Monique is tired. She studied all night.*

◊   ◊   ◊

CHORUS

MRS. SOTO

MONIQUE

ALFRED

[Monique walks into her science class.]

MRS. SOTO: Monique, you are in the wrong class.

MONIQUE: I am? What day is it?

MRS. SOTO: It's Tuesday. You have science class on Wednesday.

MONIQUE: Oh. I forgot the day. Thank you, Mrs. Soto.

CHORUS: *Monique is tired. She forgot the day.*

◊   ◊   ◊

[It is Tuesday night.]

ALFRED: Did you study for your science test tomorrow?

MONIQUE: Yes, I did. What time is it?

ALFRED: Only eight o'clock.

MONIQUE: I'm going to bed. I need to sleep.

ALFRED: Good night. Good luck tomorrow.

MONIQUE: Thanks. Good night.

Listen and Chant

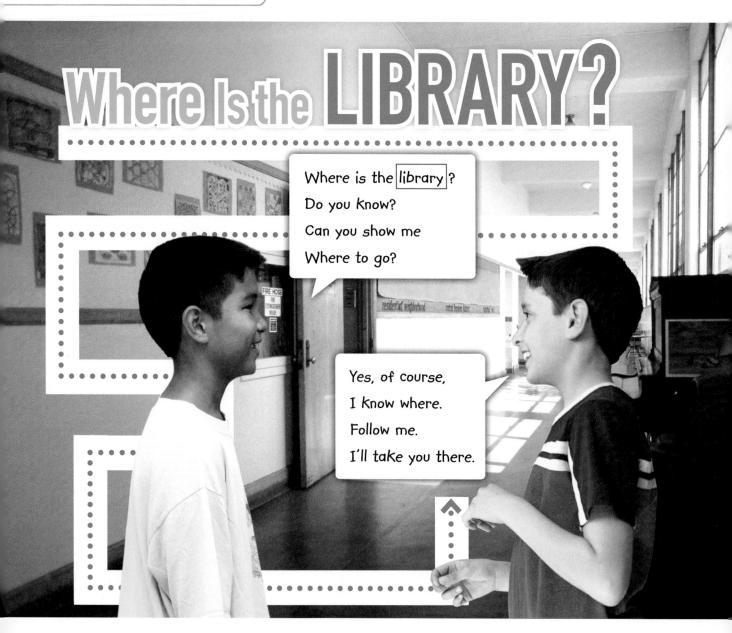

Where Is the LIBRARY?

Where is the library?
Do you know?
Can you show me
Where to go?

Yes, of course,
I know where.
Follow me.
I'll take you there.

Make your own chant.

nurse's office

main office

gym

cafeteria

School Places and Workers

🦻 Listen to your teacher.

💬 Say who each person is. Say where each person is.

1

librarian

The librarian is in the library.

2

principal

secretary

The principal and the secretary are in the main office.

Vocabulary

School Places and Workers

 Listen to your teacher.

Say who each person is. Say where each person is.

KEY WORDS

bus driver	nurse
classroom	nurse's office
counselor	parking lot
counselor's office	teacher

3

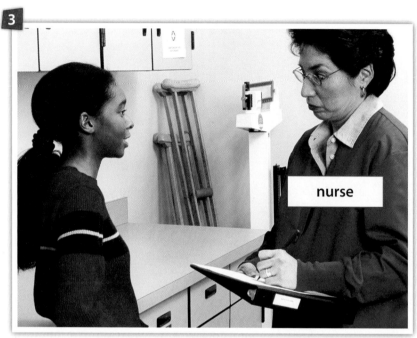

nurse

The nurse is in the nurse's office.

4

bus driver

57-92

The bus driver is in the parking lot.

5

The teacher is in the classroom.

6

The counselor is in the counselor's office.

School Places and Workers

Listen to your teacher.

Say who each person is. Say where each person is.

KEY WORDS

assistant principal	gym
auditorium	hallway
cafeteria	janitor
coach	students

7

students

The students are in the auditorium.

8

coach

The coach is in the gym.

9

janitor

The janitor is in the cafeteria.

10

assistant principal

The assistant principal is in the hallway.

Mr. Reyes is in the main office.

Use Words for School Places and Workers

✍ Draw two places in your school. Write the name of each place. Write the names of people who work there. 👥 With a partner, look at your drawings. Say the name of each person. Say where each person is.

Ask and Answer Questions

Listen and Say

Use a question like this to find out where a place is.

QUESTION	ANSWERS
Where is _____ ?	Here it is.

1

Where is the library?

Here it is.

2

Where is Room 115?

Here it is.

Say It Another Way

When you ask where something is, use **where is** or **where's**.

Where is	Where's
Where is the library?	Where's the library?
Where is the cafeteria?	Where's the cafeteria?
Where is the gym?	Where's the gym?

Shorten the two words like this:

Add '

Where is = Where's

Take out a letter.

Talk Together

Draw a map of your school on a piece of paper. Label places on your map.

Ask a partner about the places on your map.

Where is the cafeteria?

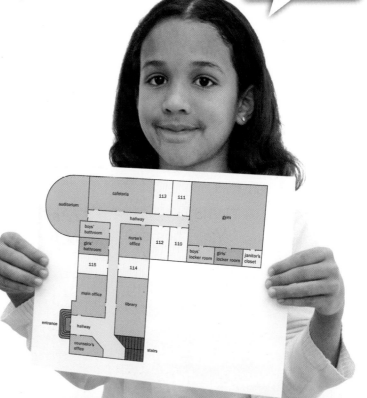

Ask and Answer Questions

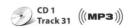

CD 1
Track 31 ((MP3))

Listen and Say

Use questions like these to ask about people.

QUESTIONS	ANSWERS
Who is the _____ ?	_____ is the _____ .
Who is _____ ?	_____ is the _____ .

1

"Who is the librarian?"

"Mrs. López is the librarian."

2

"Who is Mr. Nguyen?"

"Mr. Nguyen is the principal."

3

"Who is Ms. Thomas?"

"Ms. Thomas is the counselor."

How It Works

A **question** asks for information. Start with the word that asks for what you want to know.

Word	Asks About	Example
Who	a person	the teacher
Where	a place	the library
What	a thing	the book
When	a time	10 o'clock

Talk Together

Work with a partner. Write the names of people in your school or their roles on cards. Use the cards to ask about people.

Who is Mrs. Springer?

Mrs. Springer

High Frequency Words

Review

 Read each word aloud. Use the correct word in each sentence.

Look	What

am	is

my	I

1 _____ is on the table?

2 It _____ a book.

3 Is it _____ book?

Learn New Words

 Listen to your teacher. Say each new word.

4 **play**
Can you **play** soccer?

5 **can**
Yes, I **can** play very well.
I play soccer in P.E. class.

6 **that**
That class is my favorite.

Use New Words

Write the letters for a new word in a different order.
Your partner spells the new word.

alyp

play
p-l-a-y
play

Letters and Sounds

Spell and Read

 Look at the picture. Use your letter cards to spell the word.

Then read the word.

| i | t |

1

s _ _

h _ _

2

3

p _ _

| i | n |

4

p _ _

5

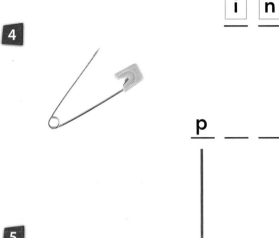

f _ _

pin
p-i-n
pin

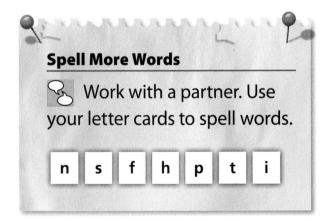

Spell More Words

Work with a partner. Use your letter cards to spell words.

| n | s | f | h | p | t | i |

Listen and Read Along

 Think about the book. What is it mainly about?

Language, Literacy & Vocabulary!

NATIONAL GEOGRAPHIC
Windows on Literacy®

Concept Book
Social Studies

Time and Routines

Cory Phillips

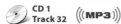

CD 1
Track 32 ((MP3))

clock

watch

March

calendar

Sunday	Monday	Tuesday	Wednesday	Thursday	Friday	Saturday
1	2	3	4	5	6	7

days of the week

January	February	March
April	May	June
July	August	September
October	November	December

year

Talk About It

1 How do people tell time?

gets up

comes home

2 What things does Pablo do at the same time every day?

eats dinner

goes to bed

Reread and Retell

3 Make two diagrams to tell about the main ideas of *Time and Routines*. Add details to each one.

4 Now use your completed main idea diagrams as you tell a partner about *Time and Routines*.

We tell time with clocks and calendars.
Clocks use hours and minutes.

We do the same things at the same time.
Pablo gets up at 7 o'clock in the morning.

Write About Your First Day in the U.S.A.

Learn About Capital Letters

Remember to start the names of cities with a **capital letter**. The names of streets also start with a capital letter.

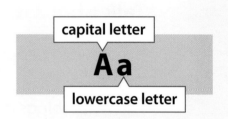

I am in Miami.

└ capital letter

I am at 349 Locust Street.

└ capital letters

The names of people and days of the week start with a capital letter. Remember that **I** is always a capital letter.

I meet Uncle Frank on Tuesday.

└ capital letters

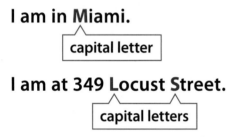 Copy the words. Use capital letters.

1 san francisco

2 main street

3 aunt natalya

4 friday

5 uncle frank

6 miami

Letters	
Aa	Nn
Bb	Oo
Cc	Pp
Dd	Qq
Ee	Rr
Ff	Ss
Gg	Tt
Hh	Uu
Ii	Vv
Jj	Ww
Kk	Xx
Ll	Yy
Mm	Zz

Study a Model

My First Day in the U.S.A.
by Marie Vincent

Tuesday, 3:00 p.m.

I am in Miami.

Tuesday, 6:30 p.m.

I am at 349 Locust Street.
I meet Uncle Frank.

Write

Now write about your first day in the U.S.A.
Draw pictures or tape photos in the boxes.
Tell where you are. Tell who you meet.

Check Your Writing

Read your work to a partner. Check the writing.
Do you need to add any capital letters?

Unit 4

Everything You Do

In This Unit

▶ **Language:** Give Information; Ask and Answer Questions

▶ **Vocabulary:** Classroom Activities; Outdoor Activities and Sports; The Arts; Pronouns

▶ **Reading:** Learn High Frequency Words; Read Decodable Text; Retell *To Be a Kid*

▶ **Writing:** Use End Marks; Write Questions and Answers

Unit Project

INTERVIEW CLASSMATES

1. Plan an interview. Write questions.

2. Do your interview. Ask questions. Take notes.

3. Write what you learned. Use sentences to tell about the person.

This is Alexandra. She can play soccer.

Alexandra Petrova

Listen and Chant

What Can You Do?

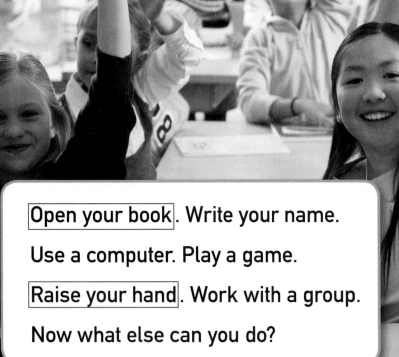

Open your book. Write your name.

Use a computer. Play a game.

Raise your hand. Work with a group.

Now what else can you do?

Make your own chant.

talk with a partner

read your book

close your book

listen to a CD

110

Words for People

🔊 Listen to your teacher.

When you talk about yourself, use **I**.

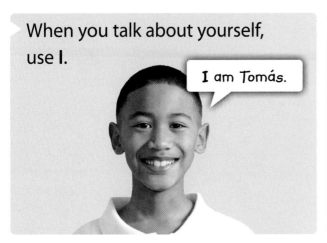

I am Tomás.

When you talk with another person, use **you**.

You are new at school. Are **you** from Mexico?

🔊 Listen to your teacher. 💬 Say each sentence.

1

I am in math class.

3

Are you in my gym class?

2

I am from Haiti.

Use Words for People

👥 Work with a partner. Say things about each other. Use the words *I* and *you*.

I am from Mexico. You are from China.

Vocabulary

Classroom Activities

 Look at each picture.

 Listen to your teacher.

 Say the name of each activity.

KEY WORDS

close your book	take out your book
listen to a CD	talk with a partner
open your book	use a computer
raise your hand	work with a group
read your book	write your name

talk with a partner

listen to a CD

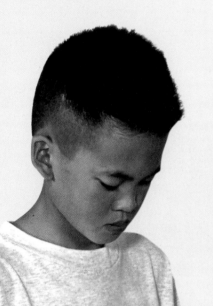

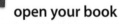
open your book

write your name

5 work with a group

8 read your book

6

close your book

9

take out your book

7
use a computer

10
raise your hand

Do Classroom Activities

Work with a partner. Say a classroom activity. Your partner will act out the activity.

Give Information

Listen and Say

Use sentences like these to talk about people.

| I am _____ . | You are _____ . |

1.

   I am a teacher.

2.

   I am in the library.

3.

   You are a student.

4.

   You are my partner.

How It Works

am	are
The verb **am** goes with **I**.	The verb **are** goes with **you**.
I am a student.	**You are** a bus driver.
I am from China.	**You are** in class.
I am at school.	**You are** from Korea.

Talk Together

 Share your information with more people in your class.

I am Jae-Min.

High Frequency Words

Review

 Read each word aloud. Use the correct word in each sentence.

Who	What

is	am

It	I

1 _____ time is it?

2 It _____ 8:40.

3 _____ is time for class.

Learn New Words

🦻 Listen to your teacher.   Say each new word.

4 **write**
My favorite class is ESL.
I learn to **write** in English.

5 **read**
I learn to **read** .

6 **answer**
I can **answer** the questions.

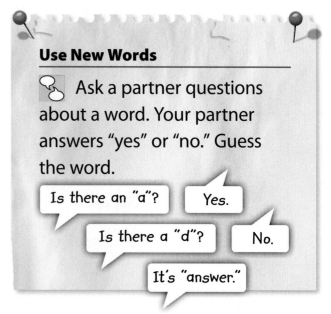

Use New Words

Ask a partner questions about a word. Your partner answers "yes" or "no." Guess the word.

Is there an "a"?   Yes.

Is there a "d"?   No.

It's "answer."

Listen and Chant

 Listen to the chant. Say the chant with your teacher.

What Time Is It?

What time is it?
What time is it?
Is it time to play?

No, it is not.
It is not time to play.
It is time to read.
It is time to write.
It is not time to play.
It is not the time.
It is not the day.
Tomorrow is the day.
Tomorrow is the day to play.

Use Letters and Sounds

How many sounds does each word have? Tell a partner.

| hit | mit | sit |

Wrap-Up

Play a Game

How to Play

1. Play with a partner.

2. Use an eraser or other small object as your game piece.

3. Put your game piece on START.

4. Flip a coin to tell how many spaces to move.

| Heads = 1 space | Tails = 2 spaces |

5. Read the sentence. Then do what it says.

> Write your name.

6. Partners take turns.

7. The first player to reach FINISH wins.

Act It Out!

START

Take out your book.

Open your book.

Read your book.

Close your book.

Write your name.

Listen to a CD.

Raise your hand.

Talk with a partner.

Use a computer.

FINISH

Listen and Chant

That Sounds Like Fun!

Ride a skateboard

in the sun.

Swim in a pool.

That sounds like fun!

Make your own chant.

| play soccer | throw a ball | walk in the park | run on a track |

Vocabulary

Words for People and Things

🦻 Listen to your teacher.

Use **he** to talk about a man or a boy.

He is the coach.

Use **she** to talk about a woman or a girl.

She is the principal.

Use **it** to talk about an animal or a thing.

This is a flag.
It is on the flagpole.

🦻 Listen to your teacher.   💬 Say each sentence.

1

He is in the park.

2

He is on the track.

3

She is a librarian.

4

It is on the field.

Use Words for People

👥 Work with a partner. Say a sentence about a person or thing in your school. Then your partner says the sentence with the word *he, she,* or *it*.

Mr. Cruz is the coach.

He is the coach.

121

Vocabulary

Outdoor Activities and Sports

👂 Listen to your teacher.

💬 Say the name of each activity.

KEY WORDS

catch a ball
kick a ball
throw a ball
play soccer
ride a skateboard

run on a track
sit in a chair
stand in line
swim in a pool
walk in the park

2 kick a ball

3 throw a ball

1 catch a ball

4 play soccer

5 ride a skateboard

6 run on a track

7 sit in a chair

8 stand in line

9 swim in a pool

10 walk in the park

Use Outdoor Activity Words

Work with a partner. Say an outdoor activity. Your partner acts out the activity.

Give Information

Listen and Say

Use sentences like these to talk about one other person or thing.

| He is _____ . | She is _____ . | It is _____ . |

1

He is a bus driver.
He is in the parking lot.

2

She is a coach.
She is in the gym.

3

Here is a ball.
It is brown.

How It Works

Use **is** with **he**, **she**, and **it**.

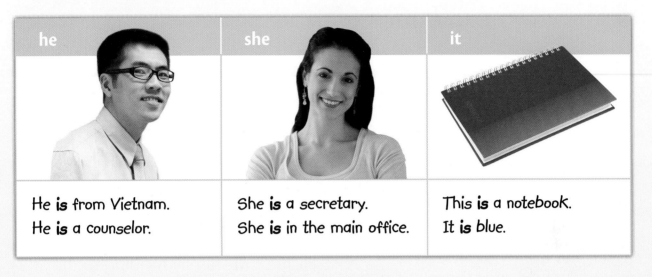

he	she	it
He **is** from Vietnam. He **is** a counselor.	She **is** a secretary. She **is** in the main office.	This **is** a notebook. It **is** blue.

Talk Together

Work with a partner. Use your picture cards from Unit 3.
Tell who each school worker is. Then tell where each worker is.

Word File Pictures
NGReach.com

He is the assistant principal.
He is in the hallway.

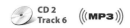
Listen and Say

People and animals can do many things. Use sentences like these to talk about things they can do.

QUESTION	ANSWERS		
Can you _____ ?	Yes, **I** can.	No, **I** cannot.	No, **I** can't.
Can Andy _____ ?	Yes, **he** can.	No, **he** cannot.	No, **he** can't.
Can Lin _____ ?	Yes, **she** can.	No, **she** cannot.	No, **she** can't.
Can a dog _____ ?	Yes, **it** can.	No, **it** cannot.	No, **it** can't.

Can You Swim?

Marc: Hi, Inez. My family is going to the lake on Saturday.

Inez: That sounds fun! Can you swim?

Marc: Yes, I can.

Inez: Can your sister swim?

Marc: No, she can't swim. She is too young.

Inez: Can the dog swim?

Marc: Yes, it can. It can swim well.

Say It Another Way

CD 2 Track 7 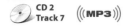 (((MP3)))

Use **cannot** or **can't** to talk about things you cannot do.

cannot	can't
I cannot throw a ball. She cannot swim.	I can't throw a ball. She can't swim.
Shorten **cannot** like this: I cannot = I can't	

Talk Together

Work with a partner. Ask your partner two questions with *can*. Your partner answers the questions. Then join another pair of students. Ask about each other and answer the questions.

Can Joe catch a baseball?

Yes, he can.

High Frequency Words

Review

🗨 Read each word aloud. Use the correct word in each sentence.

Is	Can

1 _____ you play soccer?

show	play

2 Yes, I can _____ well.

Me	My

3 _____ brother can play soccer, too.

Learn New Words

👂 Listen to your teacher.　🗨 Say each new word.

4 **boy**
Who is that boy ?

5 **he**
That is Jamal.
He plays soccer well.

6 **girl**
That girl plays well, too.

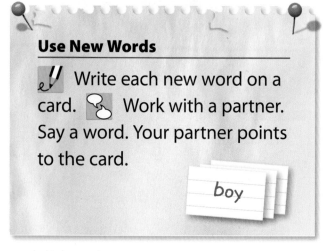

Use New Words

✏ Write each new word on a card. 🤝 Work with a partner. Say a word. Your partner points to the card.

boy

FIN FLIP

TIM HAS A SLIP.

TIM IS ON THE LIST.

☑ BEN
☑ SANDY
☑ CARL
☑ SACHI
☑ TIM
☐ LIN
☐ STEVE
☐ ROBERTA
☐ GORD

TIM AND LIN SIT. LIN HAS A PASS.

Tim, pin it on.

TIM IS IN.

This can hiss.

The fish has gills and fins.

FLIP!

IT FLIPS A FIN AT TIM!

129

Wrap-Up

Theme Theater

Juana, Brian, and Diego are at a soccer game. They are watching their friend Laura play soccer. Listen to their conversation. Then act it out.

The Soccer Game

JUANA: Where is Laura? Can you see her?

BRIAN: She is on the field.

DIEGO: I see her!

JUANA: Look at her kick the soccer ball! She scored a goal!

CHORUS: *Laura kicked the soccer ball.*
She scored a goal.

130

DIEGO: Brian, can you play soccer?

BRIAN: Yes, I can. It is fun!

DIEGO: Juana, can you play soccer?

JUANA: No, I can't. But I can ride a skateboard. That is more fun. Diego, can you ride a skateboard?

DIEGO: Yes, I can. I can play soccer, too.

CHORUS: *Brian can play soccer.*
Diego can play soccer, too.
Juana can't play soccer.
She can ride a skateboard.

◊   ◊   ◊

BRIAN: I am hungry. I want a hot dog.

JUANA: You are always hungry!

DIEGO: You can stand in line. You can buy a hot dog.

JUANA: Then you can eat.

DIEGO: Wait! Laura kicked the ball again.

JUANA: It's another goal!

CHORUS: *Laura can kick the ball!*
And Brian can eat!

131

Listen and Sing

Things We Can Do

I can sing a song.
He can act in a play.
These are things we can do every day!

We can play the drums.
It's really fun!
We do many things every day.

I can paint and draw.
She can play the guitar.
These are things we can do every day!

We all can do so many things.
We want you to join us today!

Vocabulary

Words for People

Listen to your teacher.

> When you talk about yourself and another person, use **we**.

We are in a play.

> When you talk about other people, use **they.**

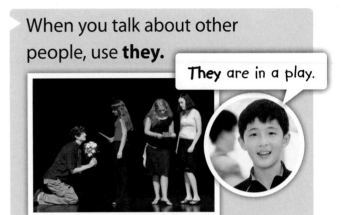

They are in a play.

Listen to your teacher. Say each sentence.

1

They are in the band.

2

We are actors.

3

We are musicians.

4

They are in the picture.

5

We are in the choir.

Use Words for People

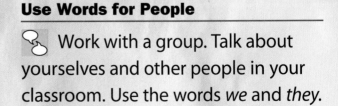

Work with a group. Talk about yourselves and other people in your classroom. Use the words *we* and *they*.

Vocabulary

The Arts

Listen to your teacher.

Say the name of each activity.

KEY WORDS

act in a play	play the guitar
dance to the music	play the piano
draw a picture	sing a song
paint a picture	take a picture
play the drums	write a story

2 dance to the music

3 draw a picture

1 act in a play

4 paint a picture

5 play the drums

6 play the guitar

7 play the piano

8 sing a song

9 take a picture

10 write a story

Use Arts Words

Work with a partner. Say an activity for the arts. Your partner acts out the activity.

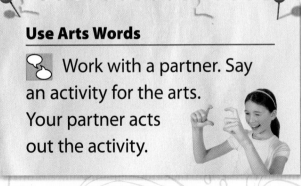

Give Information

Listen and Say

Use these words to talk about people, animals, and things.

| He is _____ . | She is _____ . | It is _____ . | They are _____ . |

1

He is a soccer player.

2

She is a janitor.

3

It is a piano.

4

They are in the gym.

5

They are red.

6

They are pets.

136

How It Works

One Person or Thing 	Sometimes you talk about only one other person or thing. Use the verb **is**.	He **is** in science class. She **is** in the auditorium. It **is** green.
More Than One Person or Thing	Other times, you talk about more than one person or thing. Use the verb **are**.	They **are** in science class. They **are** in the auditorium. They **are** green.

Talk Together

Work with a partner. Look around your classroom or school. Talk about the people and things you see. Use *he*, *she*, *it,* and *they*.

They are brown.

Give Information

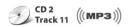

Listen and Say

Use words like these when you tell what people and things can do.

One	More Than One	One	More Than One
I can _____ .	We can _____ .	He can _____ . She can _____ . It can _____ .	They can _____ .

The Talent Show

Charlie: Hey, Vidas and Ann. There is a school talent show next month. Do you want to play in it?

Ann: Yes. We can play a song together.

Charlie: I can play the drums.

Vidas: I can play the piano.

Ann: We need a guitar player.

Vidas: I have a friend. He can play the guitar.

Ann: All our friends will watch. They can dance to the music.

Charlie: It will be fun!

How It Works

If you are not sure when to use **he**, **she**, **it**, or **they**, ask yourself these questions:

Are you talking about ...	Then use ...
one man or boy?	he
one woman or girl?	she
one thing?	it
more than one other person or thing?	they

Talk Together

Draw pictures of yourself and your friends or family. Write three things that each person can do. Work with a partner. Talk about the things you can do. Talk about the things other people can do.

Carmen is my sister. She can sing.

High Frequency Words

Review

💬 Read each word aloud. Use the correct word in each sentence.

what	day

1 It's a nice _____ today.

it	play

2 Yes, we can _____ baseball.

show	can

3 Or we _____ play soccer.

Learn New Words

👂 Listen to your teacher. 💬 Say each new word.

4 **she**
   She is Jamal's cousin.

5 **they**
   They are good.

6 **we**
   We like to watch them play.

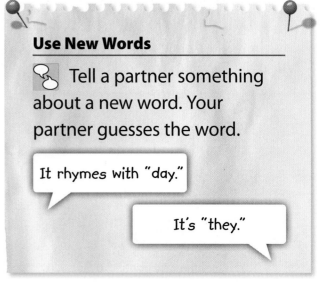

Use New Words

👂 Tell a partner something about a new word. Your partner guesses the word.

It rhymes with "day."

It's "they."

TIM SLIPS

TIM FILLS A GLASS.

TIM SIPS.

TIM WALKS.
TIM STILL SIPS.

TIM SLIPS! THE GLASS SPILLS.

THE GLASS SPILLS ON LIN'S LIST.

LIN HAS A TIP.

Tim, sit if you sip.

Listen and Read Along

 Think about the book. What is it mainly about?

To Be a Kid

Maya Ajmera and John D. Ivanko

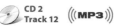 CD 2 Track 12 ((MP3))

go places

learn new things

go skating

make friends

Talk About It

1 What is the book about?

2 What kinds of things do kids like to do?

go places with family

learn things at school

play with friends

do things alone

Reread and Retell

3 Make a concept map to tell what kids do.

4 Now use your completed map as you tell a partner.

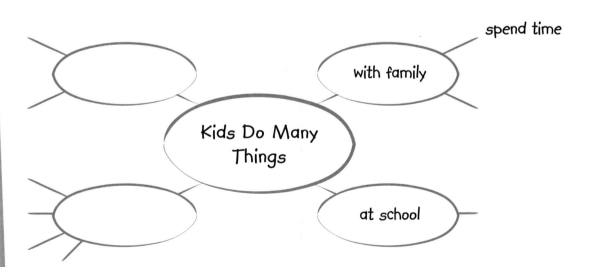

spend time

with family

Kids Do Many Things

at school

Write About a Classmate

Learn About Sentences

Use a **question mark** at the end of a question.

Can you play the guitar? < question mark

Remember to start every sentence with a **capital letter**. Put a **period** at the end of every statement.

capital letter
Can you sing?
Yes, I can. < period
capital letter

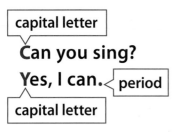 Copy each sentence. Use capital letters, periods, and question marks.

1 what is your name

2 my name is kim

3 can you play the piano

4 no, i can't

5 can you play the drums

6 yes, i can

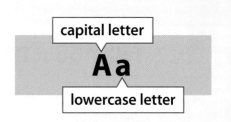

capital letter

A a

lowercase letter

Letters	
A a	N n
B b	O o
C c	P p
D d	Q q
E e	R r
F f	S s
G g	T t
H h	U u
I i	V v
J j	W w
K k	X x
L l	Y y
M m	Z z

Study a Model

An Interview with Boris Lubov

Martina: What is your name?

Boris: My name is Boris.

Martina: Where are you from?

Boris: I am from Russia.

Martina: Where do you live?

Boris: I live at 15 Oak Street.

Martina: Can you play the guitar?

Boris: No, I can't.

Martina: Can you play the drums?

Boris: Yes, I can. I can play well.

Martina: Thank you, Boris.

Boris: You're welcome.

Write

 Now write the questions and answers for your interview.

Check Your Writing

Read your work to a partner. Check the writing.
Do you need to add a question mark or a period?
Do you need to add any capital letters?

Unit 5

At Lunch

In This Unit

▶ **Language:** Give Information; Express Likes and Dislikes; Buy and Sell

▶ **Vocabulary:** Food; Money; Plurals

▶ **Reading:** Learn High Frequency Words; Learn Letters and Sounds *Rr, Dd, Cc, Vv, Oo*; Decode and Spell words with Short *o*; Summarize *Food*

▶ **Writing:** Use Plurals; Write Sentences

Unit Project

CLASS RECIPE BOOK

This is a kulich. I can show you how to make it.

1 Pick your favorite food. Learn how to make it.

2 Collect materials to show how to make it.

3 Show and tell the class how to make your favorite food.

4 Draw or take pictures. Make a class recipe book.

Listen and Chant

Tasty Treats

Buy some rice for a tasty treat.

Red chili rice is good to eat!

Buy some bread for a tasty treat.

Pita bread is good to eat!

Make your own chant.

beans

cheese

corn

Vocabulary

Food Counts

🎧 Listen to your teacher.

one | more than one

Use numbers to describe more than one thing. Often, you add **-s** to the name, too. Use **some** if you are not sure how many.

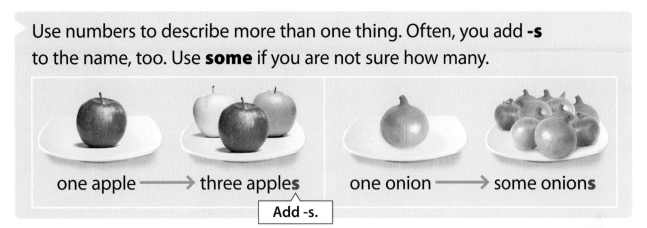

one apple ⟶ three apple**s**

one onion ⟶ some onion**s**

Add -s.

💬 Say the name of each picture. Add *-s* for more than one.

🎧 Listen to your teacher.

1

banana

some bananas

2

orange

two oranges

3

apple

three apples

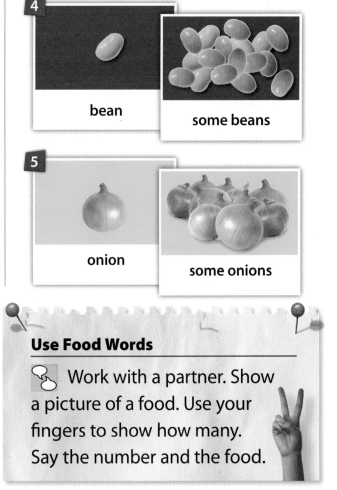

4

bean

some beans

5

onion

some onions

Use Food Words

💬 Work with a partner. Show a picture of a food. Use your fingers to show how many. Say the number and the food.

Vocabulary

Food

 Look at each picture.

 Listen to your teacher.

 Say the name of each food.

KEY WORDS

apple	lettuce
banana	milk
beans	onion
bread	orange
cheese	rice
corn	tomato

5 lettuce

1 milk

2 banana

3 rice

6 corn

7 tomato

4 cheese

8 onion

9 apple

10 orange

11 beans

12 bread

Use Food Words

You and a partner are shopping. Tell your partner what to buy.

Buy	two	
	three	
	some	_____ .
	a	
	an	
	the	

151

Give Information

Listen and Say

Use these words to point out things.

This is _____ .	That is _____ .	These are _____ .	Those are _____ .

1
What is this? This is a tomato.

3
What are these? These are tomatoes.

2
What is that? That is a tomato.

4
What are those? Those are tomatoes.

How It Works

	Close to You	Far From You
One Thing	What is this? This is _____ .	What is that? That is _____ .
More Than One Thing	What are these? These are _____ .	What are those? Those are _____ .

Talk Together

 Work with a partner. Talk about foods you see in the cafeteria.

These are apples.

High Frequency Words

Review

 Read each word aloud. Use the correct word in each sentence.

what	at

she	me

time	tomorrow

1 Is Ann _____ school?

2 No, _____ is not.

3 Call her _____ .

Learn New Words

Listen to your teacher. Say each new word.

4 **food**
This place makes the best **food** .

5 **are**
Yes. The tacos **are** very good.

6 **some**
Try **some** chips and salsa.

Use New Words

Write the letters for a new word in a different order.
Your partner spells the new word.

odof

food
f-o-o-d
food

154

Letters and Sounds

Listen and Say

👂 Listen to your teacher. 🗨 Say the name of each picture. Say the first sound.

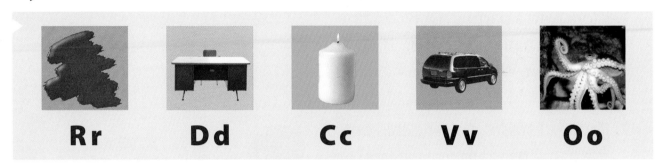

Rr	**Dd**	**Cc**	**Vv**	**Oo**

👂 Listen to each word. What letter spells the first sound you hear?

Play a Game

How to Play

1. Work with a partner. Draw a game board on a piece of paper. Then draw foods on it. Write their names.

2. Partner 1 tosses a plastic chip onto the game board to make it land on a food. Then Partner 1 asks a question about the food.

> What are those?

3. Partner 2 answers.

> Those are bananas.

4. Partner 2 tosses the plastic chip to ask about another food.

5. Partners take turns.

6. Find a new partner. Play again.

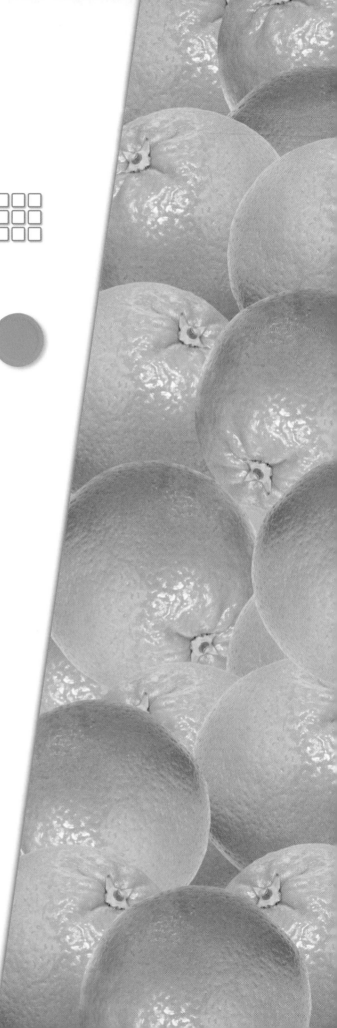

Name That Food!

Try Out Language

Listen and Chant

Foods I Like!

I like tacos.

I like cheese.

I like bok choy,

But I don't like peas!

tacos

cheese

bok choy

peas

Make your own chant.

carrots

soup

pizza

pasta

peppers

sushi

158

Food

 Listen to your teacher. Say the name of each food.

1

soup

sandwich

2

chicken

3

hot dog

4

taco

chips   salsa

5

salad

pizza

6

hamburger

7

egg

Use Food Words

Ask a partner, "What's for lunch?" Point to the food your partner names. Use words like these.

What's for	breakfast lunch dinner	?

159

Express Likes and Dislikes

Listen and Say

Use sentences like these to talk about what you like and do not like.

QUESTION	ANSWERS		
Do you like _____ ?	Yes, I like _____ .	No, I do not like _____ .	I don't like _____ .

The Hot Dog Stand

Mr. Jones: Do you like hot dogs?

Mrs. Lee: I don't know.

Marisa: Yes, I like hot dogs.

Mr. Lee: No, I do not like hot dogs. I don't like them at all!

Mr. Jones: But my hot dogs are great! Please have one.

Mrs. Lee: Yum! It's good. I like your hot dogs.

Say It Another Way

CD 2 Track 17 ((MP3))

People use many words to describe food or feelings.

	😠	😐	🙂	😋
Food	Yuck! It is awful!	So-so. It is not good.	Ok. It is good.	Yum! It's great!
Feelings	I hate it!	I don't like it.	I like it.	I love it!

Talk Together

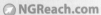 Work with a partner. Use your pictures.
Tell about foods you like and don't like.

Word File Pictures
🔵 NGReach.com

I do not like hamburgers.

161

High Frequency Words

Review

🗨 Read each word aloud. Use the correct word in each sentence.

It	I

not	name

Is	It

1 _____ like the food here.

2 I do _____ like the food there.

3 _____ is not good.

Learn New Words

👂 Listen to your teacher.   🗨 Say each new word.

4 **of**
Do you want a bowl **of** fruit?

5 **an**
No, thanks. I'll have **an** apple.

6 **a**
I'll have **a** banana.

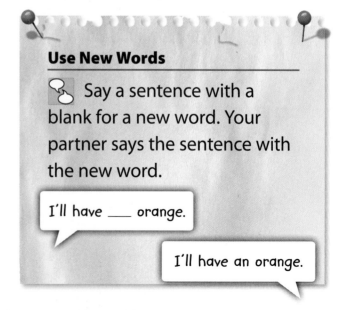

Use New Words

✋ Say a sentence with a blank for a new word. Your partner says the sentence with the new word.

I'll have ___ orange.

I'll have an orange.

Letters and Sounds

Read a Word

💬 Blend the sounds to read a word.

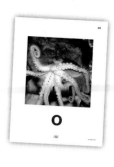

o

p
po
pot

Read More Words

💬 Read the words to a partner.

1. cot
2. hot
3. pot
4. top
5. mop

6. hop
7. pop
8. cod
9. rod

Make New Words

✏️ Use these letters. Write words on cards. 🔄 Practice reading with a partner.

r	d	c	p
h	t	m	o

cot

Theme Theater

Lydia and Marcos are buying lunch at the cafeteria. But Marcos can't decide what to eat. Listen to their conversation. Then act it out.

Pizza or Pasta?

LYDIA: Pizza or pasta? I know what I want!

MARCOS: Pizza or pasta? Hmm …

LYDIA: Oh no! Not again, Marcos!

MARCOS: What?

LYDIA: You can never choose what to eat for lunch.
We spend our whole lunchtime in line!

◊   ◊   ◊

WORKER: What can I get for you?

LYDIA: Pizza, please.

WORKER: Here you go.

◊   ◊   ◊

WORKER: What would you like?

MARCOS: Hmm …

LYDIA: Oh no! Here we go!

CHORUS: *Pizza or pasta? What will he choose?*
Can we get some pizza or pasta for you?

WORKER: Do you know what you want?

MARCOS: Lydia, what should I get?

LYDIA: Marcos, just choose the pizza. Then we can get our food and sit down.

◊   ◊   ◊

WORKER: Well?

MARCOS: I agree with Lydia. I'll have pizza today.

WORKER: Do you want cheese pizza or pepperoni pizza?

MARCOS: Cheese or pepperoni? Hmm. What should I choose?

LYDIA: Oh no! Not again.

CHORUS: *Cheese or pepperoni? He can't decide.*
Now lunchtime is over, and they're still in line!

How Much Is It ?

How much does this pasta cost?
How much is that rice?
How much does a hot dog cost?
I need to know the price.

The pasta costs four dollars.
The rice costs even more.
A hot dog is $2.50,
but it's cheaper than before.

166

Vocabulary

wallet

Money

 Listen to your teacher. Say what is in the wallet.

1

This is a one dollar bill.

2
nickel

This is ten cents.

3

This is a five dollar bill.

4

This is a twenty dollar bill.

5
dime

penny

This is eleven cents.

6
quarter

This is twenty-five cents.

7
ten dollars

one dollar

This is eleven dollars.

Use Money Words

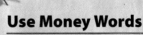 Work with a partner.
Point out bills and coins.

These are coins.

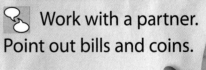

167

Listen and Say

Use sentences like these when you buy or sell things.

ONE	MORE THAN ONE
How much is _____ ?	How much are _____ ?
The _____ is _____ .	The _____ are _____ .

ONE	MORE THAN ONE
How much does it cost?	How much do they cost?
It costs _____ .	They cost _____ .

1

"How much is the hamburger?"

"The hamburger is $1.80."

2

"How much does it cost?"

"The pizza costs $16.27."

3

"How much are those fries? How much do your drinks cost?"

"The fries are 95¢. Our drinks cost 65¢ each."

Say It Another Way

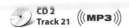

	Write It	Say It
![dollar bill, quarter, two pennies]	**dollar sign** $1.27 **decimal point**	"A dollar and twenty-seven cents" "One twenty-seven" "A buck twenty-seven"
![three quarters, dime, nickel]	**cent symbol** 65¢ $0.65	"Sixty-five cents"

Talk Together

Show your partner a picture. Your partner asks how much the food costs. Decide on a price and answer your partner.

> The apple is $0.85.

169

High Frequency Words

Review

🗨 Read each word aloud. Use the correct word in each sentence.

This	Show

name	day

He	You

1 _____ is my friend.

2 His _____ is Ron.

3 _____ is from Kenya .

Learn New Words

👂 Listen to your teacher.   🗨 Say each new word.

4 **don't**
I don't like bananas.

5 **these**
Look at these oranges.

6 **like**
Do you like oranges?

Use New Words

✍ Write each new word on a card. 👥 Work with a partner. Say a word. Your partner points to the card.

don't

Letters and Sounds

Spell and Read

👓 Look at the picture. Use your letter cards to spell the word.

🗨 Then read the word.

o p

1

m __ __

2

h __ __

3

t __ __

o t

4

c __ __

5

p __ __

cot
c–o–t
cot

Spell More Words

🗨 Work with a partner. Use your letter cards to spell words.

r d c m h p t o

Wrap-Up

Listen and Read Along

 Think about what the book is about.

CD 2
Track 22 **MP3**

corn

tomatoes

rice

salsa

172

Talk About It

1 What is the book about?

2 Where does some food come from?

farm

factory

supermarket

table

Reread and Retell

3 Make a sequence chain for *Food*. Use each box to tell about one place.

4 Now use your completed sequence chain as you tell a partner about food.

farm

↓

↓

↓

Write About Your Favorite Food

Learn About Plurals

You can count some foods, like peppers and onions.
When you name more than one, add -**s**.

1 chile pepper

3 chile peppers

✎ Copy each word. Then write the plural form.

1   banana

2   apple

3   orange

4   onion

5   egg

6   bean

Study a Model

Chalupas

I like chalupas because they are crunchy and spicy.
To make chalupas, you need:

6 tortillas
1 cup of cheese
1 can of black beans
1 tomato
1 onion
3 chile peppers
1 avocado
lettuce

Write

✍ Now write about your favorite food and what you need
to make it. Draw a picture or tape a photo of it to your page.

Check Your Writing

🗣 Read your work to a partner. Check the writing.
Do you need to add -s to make a word plural?

175

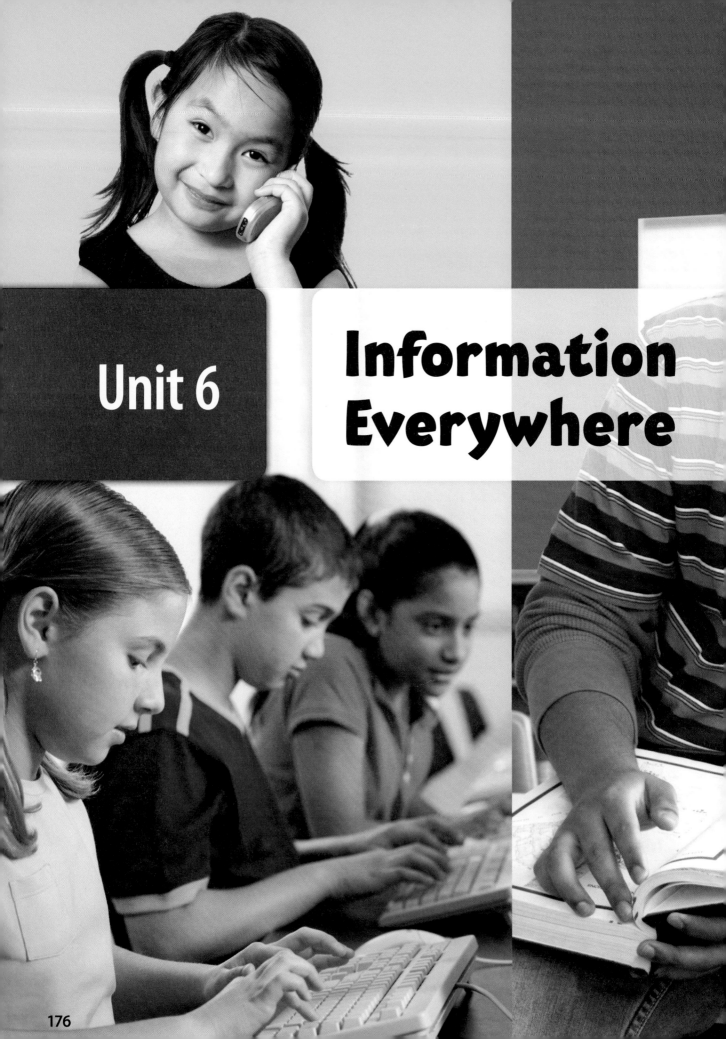

Unit 6

Information Everywhere

In This Unit

▶ **Language:** Express Needs and Wants; Give and Follow Commands

▶ **Vocabulary:** Print Materials; Parts of a Book; Technology; Computer Words; Signs and Safety; Location Words

▶ **Reading:** Learn High Frequency Words; Read Decodable Text; Retell *Good News*

▶ **Writing:** Use Periods and Exclamation Points; Write Sentences

Unit Project

MAKE A MAGAZINE

1. Work with a group. Pick a topic for a class magazine.

2. Use technology to get information. Make pages.

3. Organize the pages. Make a book.

It's on Main Street at the corner of Oak Avenue.

New sign at Main Street and Oak Avenue

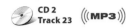
I Need Some
Information

I need a newspaper.
I need a magazine.
I need some information
About something I have seen.

I need a dictionary.
I need a textbook.
I need the meaning of a word.
Please show me where to look.

Vocabulary

Parts of a Book

🦻 Listen to your teacher.

Look for these parts at the front of a book.

cover   title page   table of contents

👀 Look at the parts of the book.   🦻 Listen to your teacher.
💬 Answer each question.

1 What is the title?

The title is _____.

2 Who is the author?

The author is _____.

3 Who is the publisher?

The publisher is _____.

4 What is the title of Chapter 2?

The title of Chapter 2 is _____.

5 On which page does Chapter 3 start?

Chapter 3 starts on page _____.

6 How many chapters are there?

There are _____ chapters.

Talk About Books

👥 Take out a book. With a partner, compare your books. Talk about the title, author, publisher, and the table of contents for each book.

179

Vocabulary

Print Materials

 Listen to your teacher.

 Say the name of each item.

KEY WORDS

advertisement	magazine
announcement	newspaper
author	page number
bulletin board	poster
chapter title	publisher
dictionary	sign
encyclopedia	stamp
envelope	textbook
letter	title

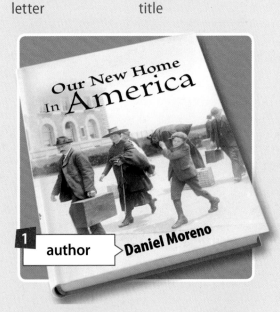

1 author   Daniel Moreno

2 title

Our New Home In America

Daniel Moreno

3 publisher

Griffin Publishers

NONFICTION

4 newspaper

5 advertisement

6 magazine

7 chapter title

CONTENTS

CHAPTER 1
Our Trip to America ... 6

CHAPTER 2
We Greet Relatives ... 12

CHAPTER 3
Our New Friends 18

CHAPTER 4
Our New Home 24

8 page number

9 sign

14 announcement

16 bulletin board

10 poster

15 letter

11 textbook

17 stamp

12 dictionary

18 envelope

13 encyclopedia

FICTION

READ

Book Club
will meet
on Thursday

A B C D E F G H I
ENCYCLOPEDIA (×9)

Talk About Print Materials

Bring an example of a print material to class. Make a class collection. Compare print materials with a partner.

Express Needs and Wants

Listen and Say

Use sentences like these to tell what you need or want.

| I need a _____ . | I need some _____ . | I want a _____ . | I want some _____ . |

1

I need a dictionary.

3

I want a book about sports.

2

I need some stamps.

4

I want some magazines about dogs.

Use the Right Word

a, an	some
Use **a** or **an** to talk about one thing that is not specific. I need **a** stamp. I need **an** envelope. I want **a** magazine.	Use **some** to talk about more than one thing. I need **some** stamps. I need **some** envelopes. I want **some** magazines.

Talk Together

Work with a partner. Use your pictures. Choose a card. Tell your partner what you want or need from the card. Use *a*, *an*, or *some*. Take turns until you use all the cards.

Word File Pictures
 NGReach.com

I need a magazine.

High Frequency Words

Review

🗨 Read each word aloud. Use the correct word in each sentence.

Show	What

a	some

an	are

1 _____ is in the library?

2 There are _____ books.

3 There _____ some magazines, too.

Learn New Words

👂 Listen to your teacher.   🗨 Say each new word.

4 **and**
I need books **and** magazines.

5 **those**
Then get these books and **those** magazines.

6 **good**
This book is very **good**.

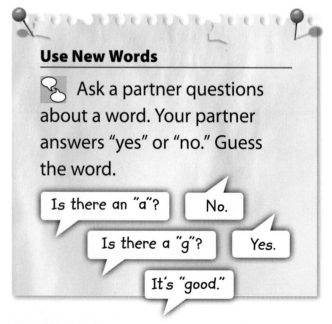

Use New Words

🗣 Ask a partner questions about a word. Your partner answers "yes" or "no." Guess the word.

Is there an "a"?   No.

Is there a "g"?   Yes.

It's "good."

Listen and Chant

 Listen to the chant. Say the chant with your teacher.

I Like Cod a Lot

I like cod a lot.
Cod and ham,
Cod and figs,
Cod and dip,
And a lot to sip.

I like cod
And a lot of dip.
I like cod
And a lot to sip.
I like cod a lot.

Use Letters and Sounds

How many sounds does each word have? Tell a partner.

| cod | dip | fig |

Wrap-Up

Play a Game

How to Play

1. Play with a partner.

1   2

2. Each partner chooses a color.

X   O

3. Partner 1 chooses a square and says a sentence.

I need some stamps.

4. If the sentence is correct, Partner 1 puts his or her sticky note in the square.

5. Partners take turns.

6. Get three marks in a row to win.

I Want _____.

I Need _____.

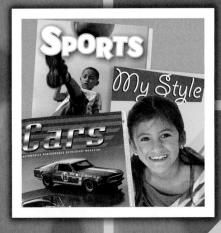

CD 2
Track 26 ((MP3))

Listen and Sing

Technology Is Good

Technology is good.
It helps us keep in touch.
So call me on your cell phone.
We can talk about so much.

Computers help us find
A lot of facts for school.
They help us write things faster.
Don't you think they're really cool?

Computer Words

👂 Listen to your teacher. 💬 Say the computer words.

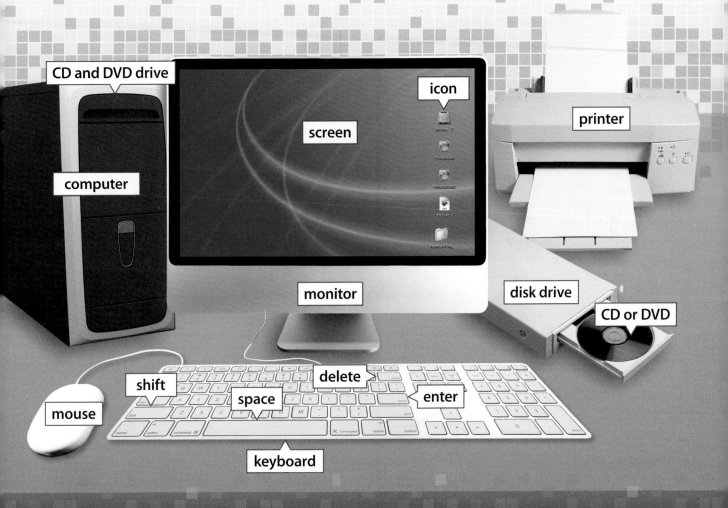

CD and DVD drive

computer

screen

icon

printer

monitor

disk drive

CD or DVD

shift

delete

space

enter

mouse

keyboard

Use Computer Words

✋ Work with a partner. Find a computer in your classroom or school. Name the parts of the computer.

189

Technology

Look at each picture.

Listen to your teacher.

Say the name of each type of technology.

1

You can use the Internet on a laptop computer.

2

You can call someone on a cell phone.

3

You can make a video with a video camera.

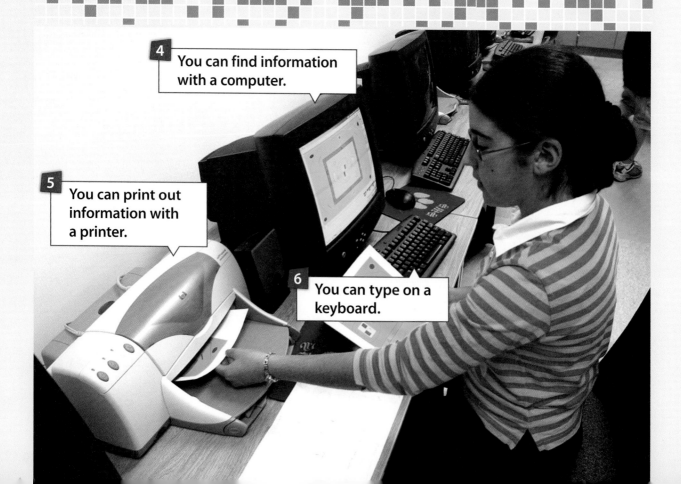

4 You can find information with a computer.

5 You can print out information with a printer.

6 You can type on a keyboard.

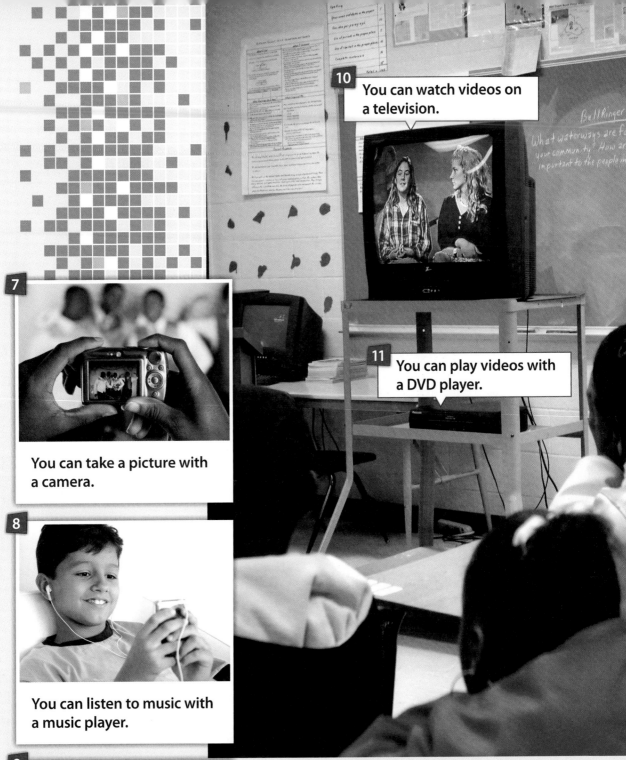

10 You can watch videos on a television.

11 You can play videos with a DVD player.

7 You can take a picture with a camera.

8 You can listen to music with a music player.

9 You can make copies with a copier.

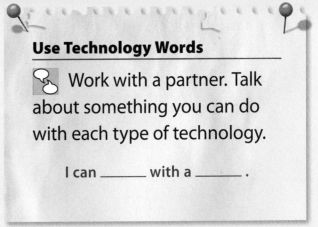

Use Technology Words

Work with a partner. Talk about something you can do with each type of technology.

I can _____ with a _____ .

191

Give and Follow Commands

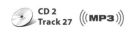
Listen and Say

When you want someone to do something, use a command.
Many commands start with these words.

call	give	listen	make	play	print	take	turn on	turn off	write

Watching a Video

Mr. Buzad: We are going to watch a video today. Listen carefully and take notes, please. Arun, please play the video.

Arun: The DVD player doesn't work.

Mr. Buzad: Turn on the DVD player.

Arun: Oh, yes.

Mr. Buzad: Thank you, Arun. Students, write your names on your papers. Please give me your notes at the end of class.

Use the Right Word

Some verbs have two words. Many two-word verbs use the word **turn**. Look at the second word to find the meaning.

turn on	turn off	turn up	turn down
Use **on** with **turn** to talk about making something start.	Use **off** with **turn** to talk about making something stop.	Use **up** with **turn** to talk about making something louder.	Use **down** with **turn** to talk about making something quieter.
Turn **on** the television.	Turn **off** the printer.	Turn **up** the music.	Turn **down** the music.

Talk Together

Work with a partner. Use your pictures. Say what you do with each thing. Then give a command. Your partner acts out the command.

Word File Pictures
NGReach.com

Turn off the television.

High Frequency Words

Review

🗨 Read each word aloud. Use the correct word in each sentence.

My	This

are	it

play	at

1 _____ is fun.

2 Yes, _____ is.

3 Let's _____ again.

Learn New Words

👂 Listen to your teacher. 🗨 Say each new word.

4 **do**
What **do** you need?

5 **book**
I need one more **book**.

6 **does**
What **does** it look like?

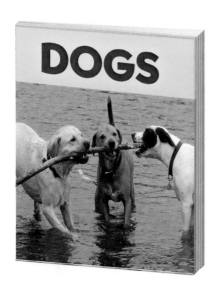

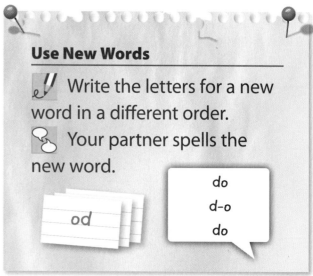

Use New Words

✏ Write the letters for a new word in a different order.
🖐 Your partner spells the new word.

od

do
d-o
do

HOT SOUP

DON HAS A LOT OF SOUP.

IT IS IN A BIG POT.

Do you like soup, Pat?

I do not like it, Don. It is hot!

NOW IT IS NOT HOT!

195

CD 2
Track 28 ((MP3))

Theme Theater

Vanna and Gustavo are planning the dance recital.

Listen to their conversation. Then act it out.

The Dance Recital

GUSTAVO: We need some signs for the dance recital.

VANNA: Here's a sign. I made it on my computer.

GUSTAVO: OK. Turn on the copier. We can make some copies.

VANNA: We can put the signs on the bulletin boards in the hallways.

GUSTAVO: That plan is great! Please make some copies.

CHORUS: *Vanna and Gustavo need some signs for the recital.*

◇   ◇   ◇

MR. LOUIS: I like the sign. When is the recital?

GUSTAVO: It is next Friday.

MR. LOUIS: Hmm. March 10 is tomorrow.

VANNA: Oh, no! I got the wrong date!

CHORUS: *The sign is great. But Vanna got the wrong date.*

CHORUS **MR. LOUIS** **GUSTAVO** **VANNA**

VANNA: I need a computer to make a new sign.
I can use the computer in the library.

MR. LOUIS: Call the librarian on my cell phone.
Ask her to meet you there.
She can help you.

VANNA: Thank you, Mr. Louis.
Gustavo, please take down
these signs. I will make new signs.

◊ ◊ ◊

GUSTAVO: We are ready for the dance recital.

VANNA: Yes, everything is ready!
We need a camera.
I want pictures of the dancers.

GUSTAVO: I have a camera.
I can take pictures.

VANNA: Great! Call me later.
Meet me before the recital.

GUSTAVO: See you later!

CHORUS: *Everything is ready!*
They are ready for the recital!

Look at the Signs

Stop! Watch out!

Don't cross the street.

Now the light is red.

You must wait to move your feet.

Look at the signs.

They're important, you know.

They tell you when to stop.

They tell you when to go.

Vocabulary

Location Words

 Listen to your teacher.

Some words help you know where something is.

The librarian is **at** the desk.

The poster is **on** the wall.

The boy is **next to** the magazines.

 Listen to your teacher. Say each sentence.

1
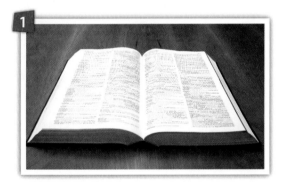
The dictionary is on the table.

3

The computer is next to the books.

2

The girl is at the desk.

Use Location Words

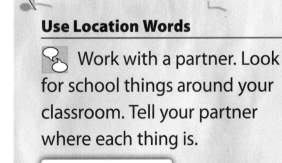 Work with a partner. Look for school things around your classroom. Tell your partner where each thing is.

> The sign is next to the door.

Vocabulary

Signs and Safety

 Look at each picture

 Listen to your teacher.

 Say the name of each sign.

KEY WORDS

bathroom sign	hospital sign
bus stop sign	railroad crossing sign
crossing sign	speed limit sign
crossing light	stop sign
exit sign	traffic light

bus stop sign

3 The bus stop sign is at the corner.

bathroom sign

1 The bathroom sign is on the door.

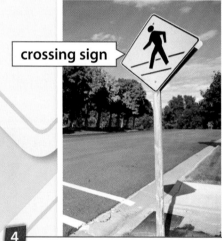

crossing sign

4 The crossing sign is next to the street.

exit sign

2 The exit sign is on the wall.

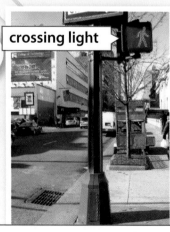

crossing light

5 The crossing light is next to the street.

hospital sign

6 The hospital sign is next to the hospital.

stop sign

9 The stop sign is at the corner.

railroad crossing sign

7 The railroad crossing sign is next to the train tracks.

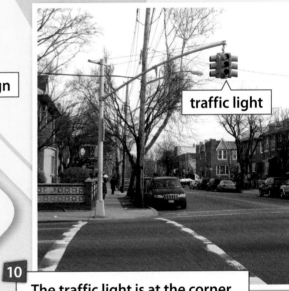

traffic light

10 The traffic light is at the corner.

speed limit sign

8 The speed limit sign is next to the school.

Use Words for Signs and Locations

Work with a partner. Look for signs around your school. Tell your partner where each sign is.

201

Give Commands

Listen and Say

Use these urgent commands to get someone to act fast.

| Be careful! | Go that way! | Help! | Hurry up! | Slow down! | Stop! | Watch out! |

1. Go that way!
Hurry up!

3. Slow down!
Be careful!

2. Stop!
Watch out!

4. Help!

202

How It Works

There are different ways to ask or tell a person what to do. Use polite commands when you can. Use urgent commands when you need to act fast.

Polite Commands	Urgent Commands

Use the word **please** at the beginning or the end.
 	
Polite commands end with a **period** (.).
 	
    Please listen to the CD.
    Listen to the CD, **please**.
	Make them short. Use your voice to show strong feeling.
	
	An urgent command ends with an **exclamation point** (!).
	
	    Stop!
	    Slow down!

Talk Together

 Work with a partner. Act out each command.

Stop!

High Frequency Words

Review

🗨 Read each word aloud. Use the correct word in each sentence.

the	do

like	show

is	book

1 What books _____ you like?

2 I _____ books about dogs.

3 Here is a good _____.

Learn New Words

👂 Listen to your teacher. 🗨 Say each new word.

4 **picture**
It has a **picture** of three dogs on it.

5 **both**
Here is one more book. Do you want **both** books?

6 **how**
Yes. **How** much are they?

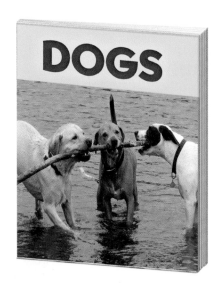

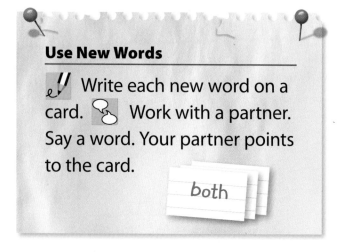

Use New Words

✏️ Write each new word on a card. 🤝 Work with a partner. Say a word. Your partner points to the card.

both

MOP TIME

SAM THE CAT IS ON THE COT.

SAM THE CAT IS OFF THE COT.

What is in the pot?

STOP SAM! DON'T HIT THE POT

THE CAT HIT THE POT. THAT IS A LOT OF SOUP.

You need a mop.

Listen and Read Along

 Think about who is in the story.

Good News

by Suzy Blackaby

 CD 2 Track 31 (((MP3)))

Ali Makki

Zeina Makki

Hassan Makki

Talk About It

1. What is the book about?

letter

phone call

2. Who got the good news first?
   How did he get it?

fax

e-mail

Reread and Retell

3. Make a sequence chain for *Good News*. Use each box to tell who got the good news.

4. Now use your completed sequence chain as you tell a partner the story.

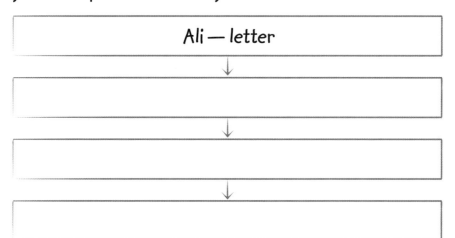

Write How to Do Something

Learn About Sentences

A **statement** tells you something. It ends with a **period**.

> I want to send an e-mail. < period

A **command** tells someone to do something. Many commands end with a **period**.

> Open your e-mail program. < period

A command that shows strong feeling ends with an **exclamation point**.

> Don't forget to click Send to send your e-mail! < exclamation point

Remember that all statements and commands begin with a capital letter.

Copy each sentence. Use capital letters, periods, and exclamation points.

1. watch out

2. please give me your phone number

3. i need to send an e-mail

4. slow down

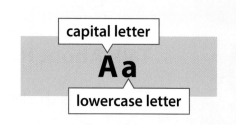

capital letter

A a

lowercase letter

Letters	
A a	N n
B b	O o
C c	P p
D d	Q q
E e	R r
F f	S s
G g	T t
H h	U u
I i	V v
J j	W w
K k	X x
L l	Y y
M m	Z z

Study a Model

How to Send an E-mail

1. Open your e-mail program.
2. Click **New** to write a new e-mail.
3. In the **To** box, type the e-mail address of the person you want to write to.
4. In the **Subject** box, type what the e-mail is about.
5. In the **message window**, type your message.
6. Don't forget to click **Send** to send your e-mail!

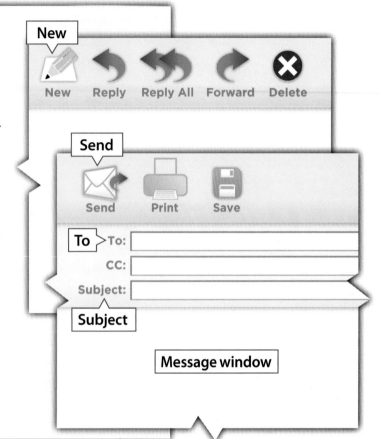

Write

Now write the steps for how to do something. Draw a picture. Label the picture.

Check Your Writing

Read your work to a partner. Check the writing. Do you need to add any capital letters? Do you need to add a period or an exclamation point?

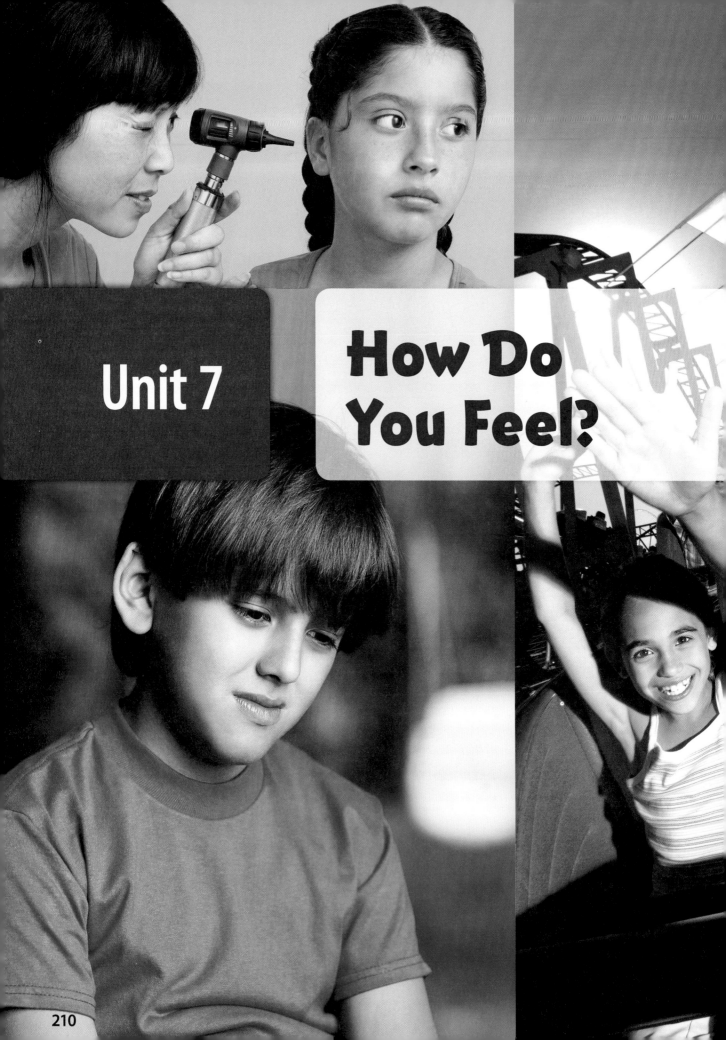

Unit 7

How Do You Feel?

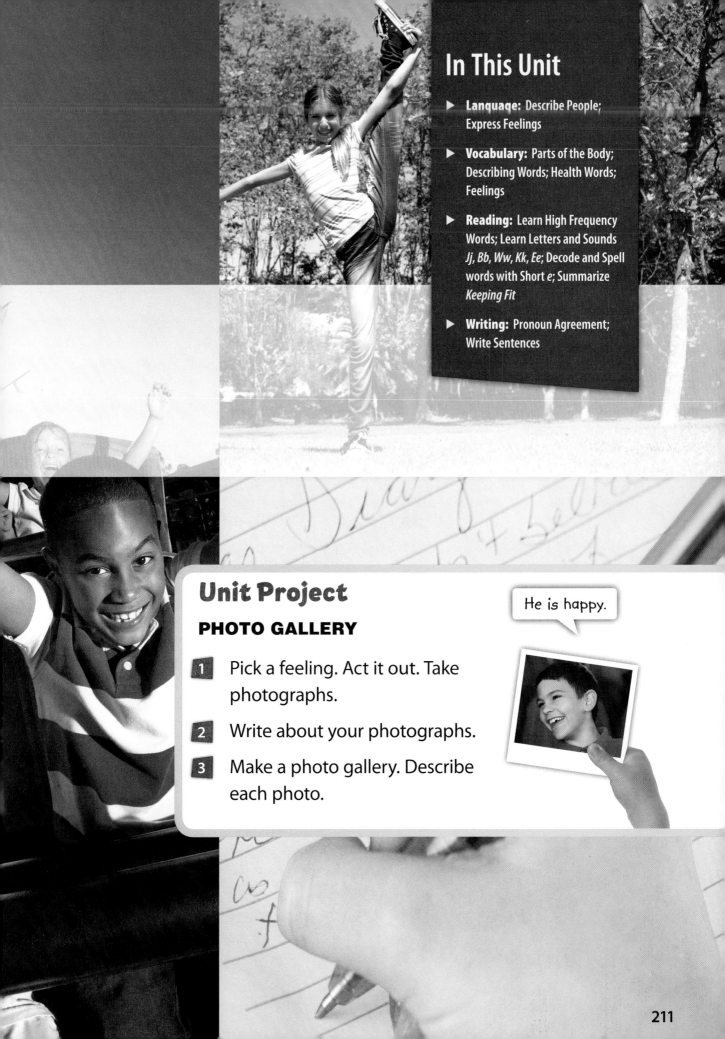

In This Unit

▶ **Language:** Describe People; Express Feelings

▶ **Vocabulary:** Parts of the Body; Describing Words; Health Words; Feelings

▶ **Reading:** Learn High Frequency Words; Learn Letters and Sounds *Jj, Bb, Ww, Kk, Ee*; Decode and Spell words with Short *e*; Summarize *Keeping Fit*

▶ **Writing:** Pronoun Agreement; Write Sentences

Unit Project

PHOTO GALLERY

He is happy.

1 Pick a feeling. Act it out. Take photographs.

2 Write about your photographs.

3 Make a photo gallery. Describe each photo.

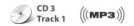
Listen and Chant

Parts of Your Body

Touch your │head│.

Point to your cheek.

Close your eyes.

Now listen to me.

Touch your │nose│.

Point to your chin.

Open your eyes.

Now do it again.

Make your own chant. Act it out.

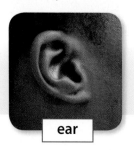

ear

face

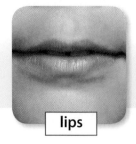

lips

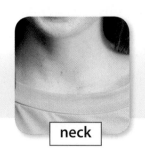

neck

hair

Parts of the Body

👓 Look at the picture.

👂 Listen to your teacher.

🗨 Say the word for each part of the body.

KEY WORDS	
cheek	head
chin	neck
eye	throat

head

eye

cheek

neck

chin

throat

Use Words for Parts of the Body

👥 Work with a partner. Point to a part of your face. Your partner says the word for the body part.

Parts of the Body

👓 Look at the picture.

👂 Listen to your teacher.

💬 Say the word for each part of the body.

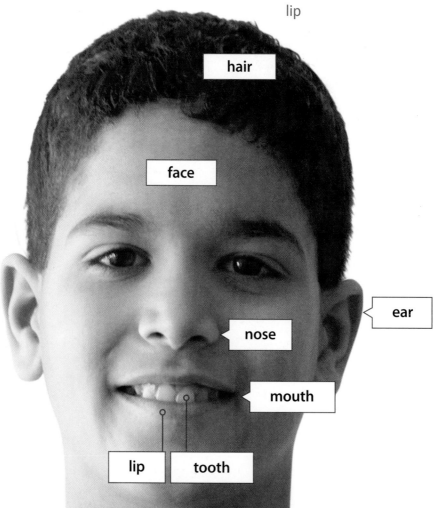

hair

face

ear

nose

mouth

lip   tooth

Use Words for Parts of the Body

💬 Work with a partner. Say a word for a body part for your face. Your partner points to that body part.

214

Describing Words

 Listen to your teacher.

Some describing words tell what a person looks like.

brown hair

long hair

a young woman

tall   short

short hair

blue eyes

an old man

 Listen to your teacher.   Say each sentence.

1

He is a young man.
He has red hair.

3
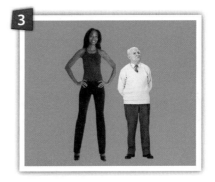

He is an old man.
He is short.

2

She is an old woman.
She has brown eyes.

Use Describing Words

Work with a partner. Use your pictures. Talk about the people. Use describing words.

She is a young woman.

182

Word File Pictures
NGReach.com

215

Describe Yourself

Listen and Say

Use sentences like these to tell what you look like.

| I am _____ . | I have _____ _____ . | My _____ is _____ .
My _____ are _____ . |

What Do You Look Like?

Uncle Tonio: Hello, Pedro. I am coming to visit you soon!

Pedro: I am happy! I will see you at the airport.

Uncle Tonio: Tell me what you look like now.

Pedro: Well, I am tall. My hair is brown. And I have brown eyes. What do you look like?

Uncle Tonio: I am tall, too. I have gray hair. And my eyes are blue.

Pedro: OK. See you soon, Uncle Tonio! Have a safe trip!

How It Works

Use **I** to talk about yourself.
Use **my** to tell about something you own.

I ⟶ my

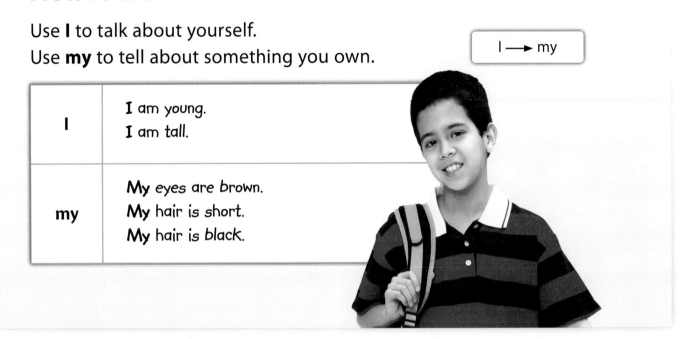

I	I am young. I am tall.
my	My eyes are brown. My hair is short. My hair is black.

Talk Together

Work with a partner. Tell your partner what you look like. Then tell another partner.

I have brown hair.
My eyes are brown.

Describe Other People

Listen and Say

Use sentences like these to tell what other people look like.

He is _____ .	He has _____ _____ .	His _____ is _____ .	His _____ are _____ .
She is _____ .	She has _____ _____ .	Her _____ is _____ .	Her _____ are _____ .

Waiting for Friends

Pilar: Hi, Michael. What are you doing?

Michael: I am waiting for my friends, Paulo and Stacey. We are going to see a movie.

Pilar: Oh. What does Paulo look like?

Michael: He is tall. He has short hair. His eyes are brown.

Pilar: OK. What does Stacey look like?

Michael: She is short. She has black hair. Her hair is long.

Pilar: Oh, I see them. Here they come now!

How It Works

Use **he** to talk about a man or a boy. Use **his** to talk about something he owns.
Use **she** to talk about a woman or a girl. Use **her** to talk about something she owns.

```
he ——▸ his
she ——▸ her
```

Man or boy	he	He is old.
	his	His eyes are brown.
Woman or girl	she	She is young.
	her	Her eyes are green.

Talk Together

Work with a partner. Find pictures of people in magazines or a newspaper. Tell your partner what each person looks like.

Same old classes?
Same old friends?
Same old life?
BREAK AWAY IN
MIRO JEANS!
The look is unforgettable. The fit is unforgivable.

Review

🗨 Read each word aloud. Use the correct word in each sentence.

How	That

day	like

don't	does

1 _____ food looks good.

2 I don't _____ milk.

3 Then _____ get it.

Learn New Words

👂 Listen to your teacher.   🗨 Say each new word.

4 **old**
My grandfather is **old**.

5 **has**
He **has** gray hair.

6 **get**
He needs to **get** new glasses.

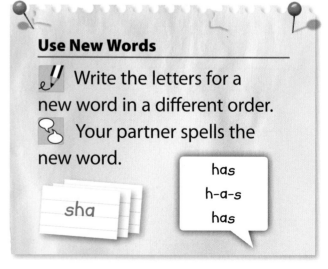

Use New Words

✏ Write the letters for a new word in a different order.

🗨 Your partner spells the new word.

sha

has
h-a-s
has

Letters and Sounds

Listen and Say

Listen to your teacher. Say the name of each picture. Say the first sound.

| Jj | Bb | Ww | Kk | Ee |

Listen to each word. What letter spells the first sound you hear?

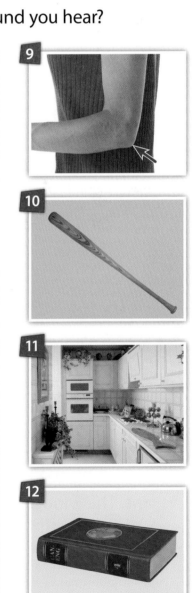

Play a Game

How to Play

1. Play with a partner.

2. Use two plastic chips as markers.

3. Partner 1 tosses a plastic chip onto Board 1. Then Partner 1 tosses another plastic chip onto Board 2. Partner 1 uses the two words in a sentence.

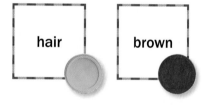

> Her hair is brown.

> She has a little nose.

4. Then Partner 1 draws the body part.

5. Partner 2 takes a turn.

6. A person who lands on a body part that he or she has already drawn loses a turn.

7. The first person to draw a complete face wins. The winner describes the face.

> She has green eyes.
> Her hair is brown.

Draw a FACE

Parts of the Body

Board 1	cheeks	chin	ears	eyes
	hair	head	mouth	neck	nose

Board 1	cheeks	chin	ears	eyes
hair	head	mouth	neck	nose

Describing Words

Board 2	big	little	short	long
blue	black	brown	green	red

Listen and Chant

HOW DO YOU FEEL?

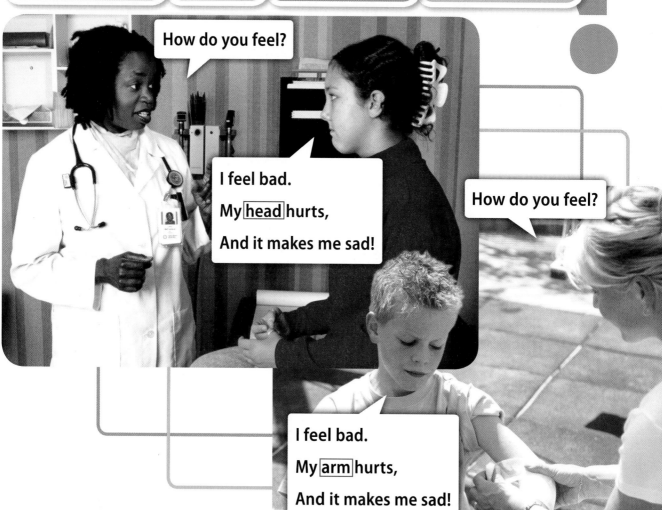

How do you feel?

I feel bad.
My head hurts,
And it makes me sad!

How do you feel?

I feel bad.
My arm hurts,
And it makes me sad!

Make your own chant.

stomach

hand

back

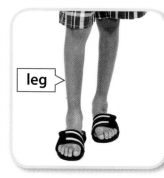

leg

Health Words

 Listen to your teacher.

Sometimes you feel bad because you have:

a headache

a toothache

a fever

an earache

a sore throat

a cold

 Listen to your teacher. Say each sentence.

1 My head is hot.
I have a fever.

2 My throat hurts.
I have a sore throat.

3 My tooth hurts.
I have a toothache.

4 My ear hurts.
I have an earache.

5 My nose hurts.
I have a cold.

6 My head hurts.
I have a headache.

Use Health Words

Work with a partner. Read the sentences on this page. Act out how you feel.

Vocabulary

Parts of the Body

Look at each picture.

Listen to your teacher.

Say the name of each body part.

KEY WORDS

ankle	hip
arm	knee
back	leg
body	shoulder
chest	stomach
elbow	thumb
finger	toe
foot	wrist
hand	

1 arm

2 chest

3 stomach

4 hip

5 leg

6 knee

7 shoulder

8 elbow

9 back

10 body

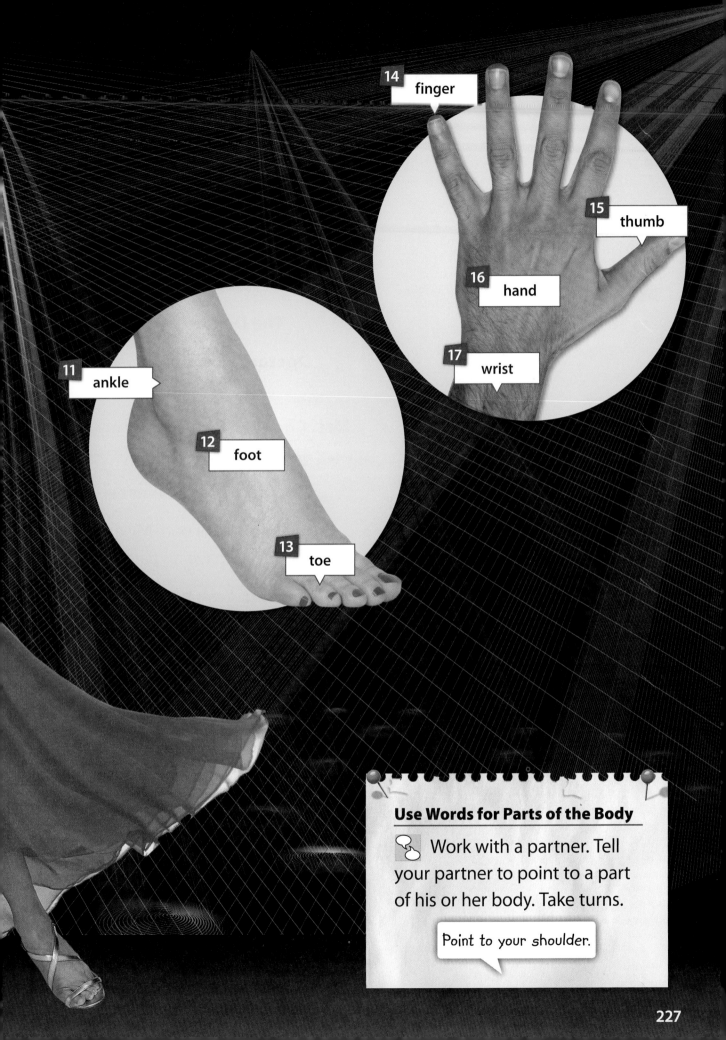

14 finger
15 thumb
16 hand
17 wrist
11 ankle
12 foot
13 toe

Use Words for Parts of the Body

Work with a partner. Tell your partner to point to a part of his or her body. Take turns.

Point to your shoulder.

Express Feelings

Listen and Say

Use sentences like these to tell how you feel.

QUESTION	ANSWERS			
How do you feel?	I feel fine.	I feel bad.	My _____ hurts.	I have a _____ .

The Doctor's Office

Doctor: How do you feel, Mrs. Cheng?

Mrs. Cheng: I feel fine. But my son Lee feels bad.

Doctor: How do you feel, Lee?

Lee: I feel bad. My ear hurts. I have an earache.

Doctor: I can help you. Come with me. I need to look in your ear.

Say It Another Way

There are many ways to say how you feel.

 When You Feel Good	When You Feel Bad
I feel good. I feel fine. I'm OK. I feel great!	I feel bad. I don't feel well. I'm sick. I feel terrible!

Talk Together

Work with a partner. Use your pictures. Choose a picture card. Ask your partner, "How do you feel?" Your partner answers.

Word File Pictures
NGReach.com

How do you feel?

I feel bad.
My back hurts.

229

High Frequency Words

Review

Read each word aloud. Use the correct word in each sentence.

how	has

old	that

get	girl

1 My sister _____ eye glasses.

2 They are _____ .

3 She will _____ new glasses.

Learn New Words

Listen to your teacher.   Say each new word.

4 **call**
My mother will **call** the eye doctor.

5 **have**
Now we **have** new glasses.

6 **great**
The new glasses are **great**!

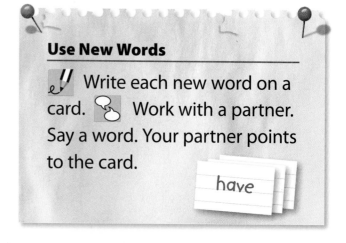

Use New Words

Write each new word on a card.   Work with a partner. Say a word. Your partner points to the card.

have

Letters and Sounds

Read a Word

 Blend the sounds to read a word.

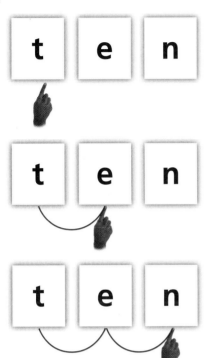

t
te
ten

Read More Words

Read the words to a partner.

1 Jen
2 Ben
3 hen
4 ten
5 Ken

6 jet
7 bet
8 net
9 wet

Make New Words

Use these letters. Write words on cards. Practice reading with a partner.

j	b	w	k
t	h	n	e

hen

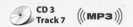

CD 3
Track 7 MP3

Theme Theater

Juanita is at the doctor's office with her mother. Listen to
their conversation. Then act it out.

At the Doctor's Office

DR. SMITH: Hello, Juanita. Hello, Mrs. Campos.

MRS. CAMPOS: Hello, Dr. Smith.

JUANITA: Hi, Dr. Smith.

DR. SMITH: You look sick, Juanita. How do you feel?

JUANITA: I feel bad.

◊   ◊   ◊

DR. SMITH: I'm sorry to hear that. Tell me more.

JUANITA: My ear hurts. I feel terrible!

MRS. CAMPOS: She has a fever.

CHORUS: *Juanita feels terrible!*
She has a fever.

CHORUS   MRS. CAMPOS   JUANITA   DR. SMITH

JUANITA: I want to feel better, Dr. Smith. I want to play soccer on Saturday.

MRS. CAMPOS: She needs some medicine.

DR. SMITH: I will give you medicine. It will help your earache and fever.

JUANITA: Can I play soccer on Saturday?

DR. SMITH: Yes, you can. Go home and rest. Drink lots of water. Take the medicine. You will feel better soon.

CHORUS: *Juanita will feel better soon. She can play soccer on Saturday.*

◊   ◊   ◊

MRS. CAMPOS: Thank you, Dr. Smith.

DR. SMITH: You're welcome. Have a nice day.

JUANITA: Good-bye, Dr. Smith.

CHORUS: *Juanita will feel better soon. They say "good-bye" and "thank you."*

233

Listen and Sing

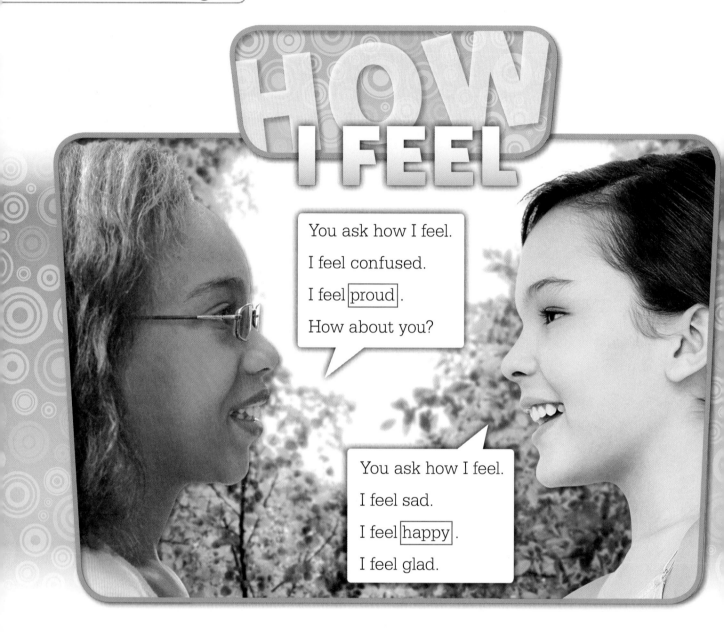

HOW I FEEL

You ask how I feel.
I feel confused.
I feel proud.
How about you?

You ask how I feel.
I feel sad.
I feel happy.
I feel glad.

Make your own song.

surprised

scared

angry

Vocabulary

Feelings

 Listen to your teacher. Say each sentence.

1

I am scared.

2

I am sad.

3

I am bored.

4

I am happy.

5

I am confused.

6

I am surprised.

7

I am proud.

8

I am angry.

Use Words for Feelings

Work with a partner. Write the feelings on cards. Choose a card. Act out the feeling. Your partner guesses the feeling.

surprised

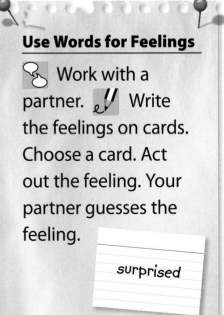

235

Express Feelings

Listen and Say

Use sentences like these to tell how you feel.

QUESTION	ANSWERS	
How do you feel?	I am _____ .	I feel _____ .

First Place

Clara: How do you feel?

Isabel: I feel happy. Our team won the game! We got first place!

Clara: I am proud.

Isabel: I am surprised. I did not think we would win.

Clara: But we have a great team!

236

Say It Another Way

 CD 3
Track 10 (((MP3)))

People use different words to describe the same feeling.

Feeling	😊 happy	😞 sad	😮 scared	😠 angry
Other Words	glad pleased	unhappy	afraid frightened	mad upset

Talk Together

Work with a partner. Ask, "How do you feel?" Your partner answers and acts out the feeling.

High Frequency Words

Review

💬 Read each word aloud. Use the correct word in each sentence.

are	look

has	am

have	read

1 Hello. How _____ you?

2 I _____ not fine.

3 I _____ a headache.

Learn New Words

👂 Listen to your teacher. 💬 Say each new word.

4 **feel**
How do you feel?

5 **very**
I am very sick.

6 **too**
I feel bad, too.

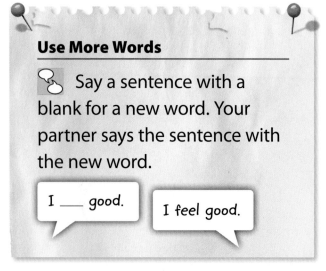

Use More Words

🗣 Say a sentence with a blank for a new word. Your partner says the sentence with the new word.

> I ___ good.

> I feel good.

238

Letters and Sounds

Spell and Read

 Look at the picture. Use your letter cards to spell the word.

Then read the word.

| e | n |

1

t _ _

2

h _ _

3

p _ _

| e | t |

4

j _ _

5

w _ _

hen
h-e-n
hen

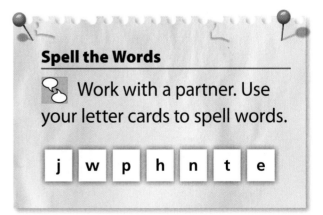

Spell the Words

Work with a partner. Use your letter cards to spell words.

| j | w | p | h | n | t | e |

239

Wrap-Up

Listen and Read Along

 Think about the book. What is it about?

Language, Literacy & Vocabulary!

NATIONAL GEOGRAPHIC
Windows on Literacy®

Concept Book
Social Studies

Keeping Fit

Zeina Mahran

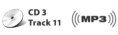
CD 3
Track 11 ((MP3))

play basketball

play

skate

play soccer

Talk About It

1 How do people keep fit?

eat right

sleep

2 What kinds of ways can people exercise?

exercise

Reread and Retell

3 Make a concept map to tell about how people keep fit.

4 Now use your completed concept map as you tell a partner about *Keeping Fit*.

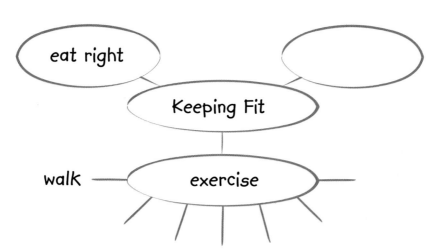

eat right

Keeping Fit

walk — exercise

Writing

Describe a Friend

Learn About Words for People

Use **he** and **his** when talking about a man or a boy.
Use **she** and **her** when talking about a woman or a girl.

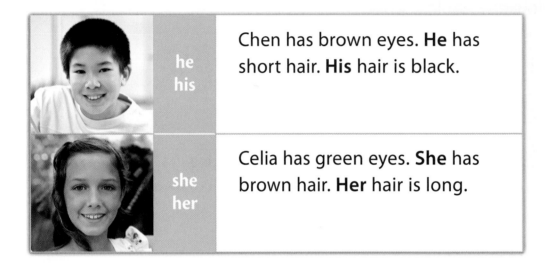

	he **his**	Chen has brown eyes. **He** has short hair. **His** hair is black.
	she **her**	Celia has green eyes. **She** has brown hair. **Her** hair is long.

Copy each sentence. Then add the word that finishes the sentence.

1. Juan has short hair.
   _____ has brown eyes.

2. Sarah has blue eyes.
   _____ hair is red.

3. Victor has blonde hair.
   _____ eyes are green.

4. Carina has brown eyes.
   _____ has long hair.

5. Ana has long hair.
   _____ has brown eyes.

6. Jon has short hair.
   _____ eyes are brown.

Study a Model

Maria has green eyes.

Her hair is red.
She has long hair.

This is Maria!

Write

Now write about a friend. Draw pictures or tape photos of your friend to your page.

Check Your Writing

Read your work to a partner. Check the writing. Did you use *he* or *his* to describe a man or a boy? Did you use *she* or *her* to describe a woman or a girl?

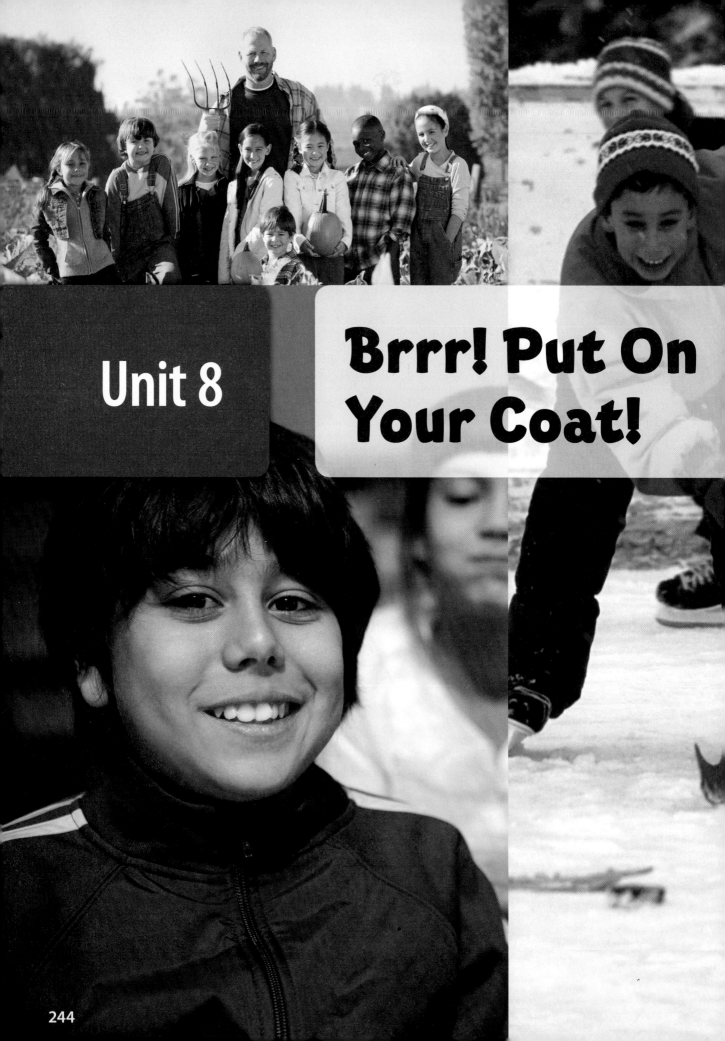

Unit 8

Brrr! Put On Your Coat!

In This Unit

▶ **Language:** Ask and Answer Questions; Describe Things; Express Ideas

▶ **Vocabulary:** Clothing; Time Order Words; Describing Words; Weather

▶ **Reading:** Learn High Frequency Words; Read Decodable Text; Summarize *Shoes, Shoes, Shoes*

▶ **Writing:** Use Periods and Exclamation Points; Write a Letter and a List

Unit Project

DESIGN CLOTHES

1 Pick a piece of clothing.

2 Describe your plans. Design the clothing.

3 Show your design. Tell about it.

> Here are some jeans. They have beads.

The Clothing MACHINE

Socks and shoes,
Jackets and jeans,
Shirts and skirts,
I'm a clothing machine!

Make your own song.

pants

belts

dresses

sweaters

Vocabulary

Clothing

👂 Listen to your teacher.

🗨 Say the name of each piece of clothing.

KEY WORDS

collar   skirt

dress   sweater

jacket

2 collar

3 jacket

1 dress

4 sweater

5 skirt

Clothing

🦻 Listen to your teacher.

🗨 Say the name of each piece of clothing.

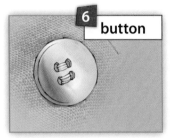

6 button

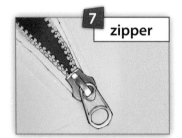

7 zipper

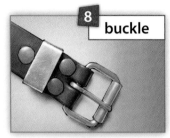

8 buckle

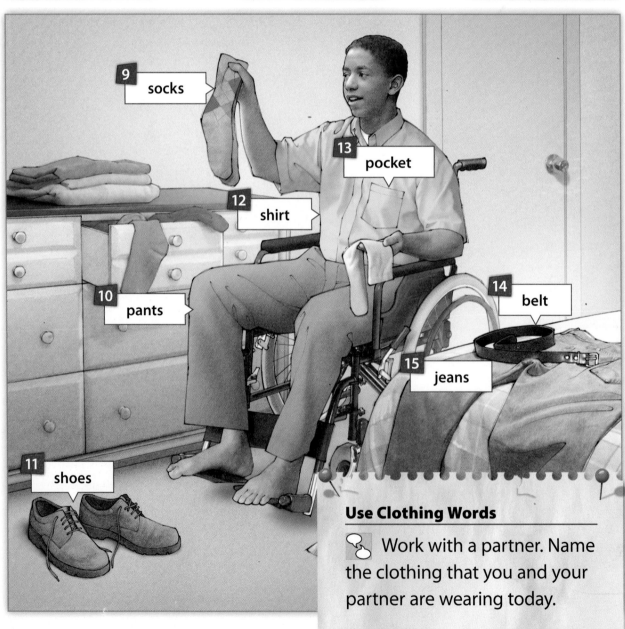

9 socks

13 pocket

12 shirt

10 pants

14 belt

15 jeans

11 shoes

Use Clothing Words

🗨 Work with a partner. Name the clothing that you and your partner are wearing today.

Time Order Words

 Listen to your teacher.

Use these words to put actions in order.

   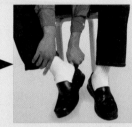

First, I put on my shirt.　**Next**, I put on my jeans.　**Then**, I put on my socks.　**Last**, I put on my shoes.

 Listen to your teacher.　 Say each sentence.

First, I put on my shirt.　Next, I put on my jeans.　Then, I put on my belt.　Last, I put on my sweater.

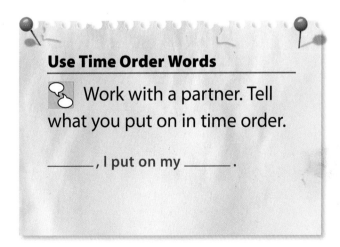

Use Time Order Words

Work with a partner. Tell what you put on in time order.

_____, I put on my _____.

249

Ask and Answer Questions

Listen and Say

Use questions like these to find out information.

QUESTIONS	ANSWERS		
Does the _____ have _____ ?	Yes, it does.	No, it does not.	No, it doesn't.
Do the _____ have _____ ?	Yes, they do.	No, they do not.	No, they don't.

A Shirt and Shoes for Uncle Guillermo

Domingo: Here's the shirt for Uncle Guillermo.

Mom: Does the shirt have a collar?

Domingo: Yes, it does. He likes shirts with collars.

Mom: OK. Does the shirt have a pocket?

Domingo: No, it doesn't. Now look at these shoes.

Mom: Do the shoes have buckles?

Domingo: No, they don't. Here, look at them.

Mom: Oh, yes. Uncle Guillermo will like them!

Say It Another Way

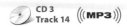

	does not / do not	doesn't / don't
When you talk about one thing, use **does not** or **doesn't**. Take out a letter. → Add an '. does nøt = doesn't	The shirt **does not** have a pocket. The sweater **does not** have buttons.	The shirt **doesn't** have a pocket. The sweater **doesn't** have buttons.
When you talk about more than one thing, use **do not** or **don't**. Take out a letter. → Add an '. do nøt = don't	The shirts **do not** have pockets. The sweaters **do not** have zippers.	The shirts **don't** have pockets. The sweaters **don't** have zippers.

Talk Together

Work with a partner. Look at pictures of clothing in magazines. Take turns asking and answering questions about the clothing.

Does the shirt have a collar?

Yes, it does.

High Frequency Words

Review

🗨 Read each word aloud. Use the correct word in each sentence.

feel	my

Read	Do

look	have

1 I _____ cold.

2 _____ you have a sweater?

3 Yes, I do. I _____ a jacket, too.

Learn New Words

👂 Listen to your teacher. 🗨 Say each new word.

4 **your**
Put **your** sweater on.

5 **things**
Do these **things** before you go home.

6 **put**
Put your jacket on. Put your hat and gloves on, too.

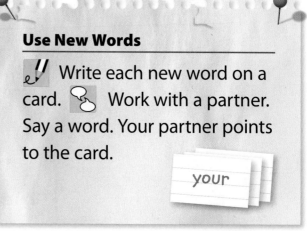

Use New Words

✏ Write each new word on a card. 🗨 Work with a partner. Say a word. Your partner points to the card.

your

252

Listen and Chant

 Listen to the chant.   Say the chant with your teacher.

How Are You, Jen?

How are you, Jen?
How are you, Kit?

    We feel great!
    We feel fit!

If we get sad,
We hop on the mat.
We tag, we kid,
We do the jig.

    If we get mad,
    We jab at the bag.
    We bat, we hit,
    And we feel very fit!

Use Letters and Sounds

How many sounds does each word have? Tell a partner.

bag

hop

jig

Play a Game

How to Play

1. Draw a game board on a piece of paper. Then draw a different piece of clothing in each square.

2. Use plastic chips as markers.

3. Your teacher says the name of a piece of clothing.

Shirt

4. If the clothing is on your game board, put a marker on the square.

5. When you have three markers in a row, call out, "I'm ready!"

6. Other students ask questions about the clothing in your row.

Does the shirt have a collar?

7. If you answer the questions correctly, you win. If not, take away the markers and keep playing.

I'm Ready!

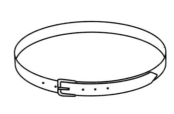

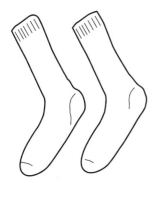

Listen and Chant

READY TO GO!

Zip up those cool boots.

Put on your brown jacket.

Get your hat.

Grab your gloves.

Tie your scarf.

Get all snug.

Time to go to school.

Clothing

Listen to your teacher.

Say the name of each piece of clothing.

boots	hat
coat	mittens
gloves	scarf

hat

scarf

mittens

coat

gloves

boots

Use Clothing Words

Work with a partner. Say a word for a piece of clothing. Your partner points to that piece of clothing in the picture.

Vocabulary

Clothing

👂 Listen to your teacher.

💬 Say the word for each piece of clothing.

KEY WORDS

sandals	strap
shorts	stripe
sneakers	T-shirt

T-shirt

stripe

shorts

sandals

sneakers

strap

Use Clothing Words

💬 Work with a partner. Say a word for a piece of clothing. Your partner points to that piece of clothing in the picture.

258

Vocabulary

Describing Words

 Listen to your teacher.

Describing words can tell what something looks like or how it feels.

Colors and Sizes	Textures	Kinds
 a small, yellow T-shirt	 soft mittens  smooth boots	 a shirt with long sleeves a warm scarf

 Listen to your teacher. Say each sentence.

1

This is a large, blue sweater.

2

I need a shirt with short sleeves.

3

I want some smooth boots with a low heel.

Use Describing Words

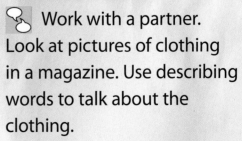 Work with a partner. Look at pictures of clothing in a magazine. Use describing words to talk about the clothing.

259

Describe Things

Listen and Say

Use sentences like these to name something and tell what it is like.

Here is a _____ . It has _____ .	Here are some _____ . They have _____ .

1

Here is a shirt.
It has short sleeves.

2

Here are some sneakers.
They have red stripes.

260

How It Works

When you describe one thing, use **has**.

The *boot* **has** a high heel.

The *shirt* **has** white stripes.

When you describe more than one thing, use **have**.

The *boots* **have** high heels.

The *shirts* **have** short sleeves.

When you describe jeans, pants, and shorts, use **have**.

The *jeans* **have** two pockets.

The *pants* **have** a zipper.

The *shorts* **have** blue stripes.

Talk Together

Draw a game board of nine spaces. Then draw a picture of clothing in each space. Use different colors. Choose a mark: X or O. Describe the clothing in a space. Then draw your mark on the space. Take turns with a partner. Get three Xs or Os in a row to win.

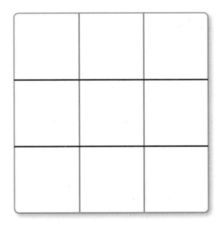

Ask and Answer Questions

Listen and Say

Use sentences like these to tell which thing you like.

QUESTION	ANSWERS	
Which _____ do you like?	I like this _____ . I like that _____ .	I like these _____ . I like those _____ .

Shopping for Clothes

Rebecca: I like these shirts. Which shirt do you like, Jen?

Jen: I like that shirt. Gina, which shirt do you like?

Gina: I like this shirt. It is blue.

Jen: They are both nice.

Rebecca: Which shirt will you buy?

Jen: I will buy the blue one. I need a blue shirt.

Use the Right Word

You can use the words **which** and **what** to ask questions.

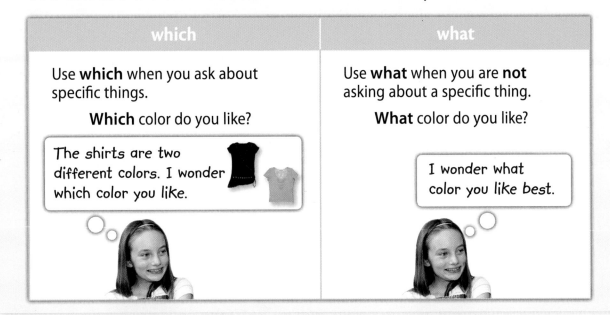

which	what
Use **which** when you ask about specific things. **Which** color do you like? The shirts are two different colors. I wonder which color you like.	Use **what** when you are **not** asking about a specific thing. **What** color do you like? I wonder what color you like best.

Talk Together

Work with a partner. Look in a clothing catalog. Talk about the clothing. Ask your partner which clothing he or she likes. Your partner points to the clothing and answers the question.

Which shoes do you like?

I like these shoes.

High Frequency Words

Review

🗨 Read each word aloud. Use the correct word in each sentence.

has	have

Does	Do

and	too

1 I _____ my cell phone.

2 _____ you have a pen?

3 Yes. I have paper, _____ .

Learn New Words

👂 Listen to your teacher.   🗨 Say each new word.

4 **help**
I need your **help**.

5 **group**
A **group** of my friends
will come.

6 **with**
Can you work **with** us?

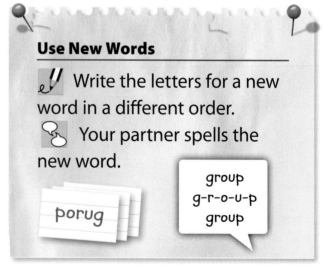

Use New Words

✏️ Write the letters for a new word in a different order.
🗨 Your partner spells the new word.

porug

group
g-r-o-u-p
group

264

GET IN BED, KEN

Are you sick, Ken?

I do not feel well.

You are ill, Ken. Get in bed.

Let me help you get well.

Set this on the hot spot. It is wet.

IT IS TEN O'CLOCK....

I bet you feel better, Ken.

I feel better, Jen, but my bed is a mess!

Theme Theater

Fernando and Myra are shopping for a gift for Silvia. Silvia is Fernando's sister. Listen to their conversation. Then act it out.

Sneakers for Silvia

FERNANDO: It's my sister Silvia's birthday. What can I buy?

MYRA: What does she want?

CHORUS: *What does Silvia want?*

FERNANDO: She wants some sneakers.

MYRA: Great! Here are the shoes for women.

SALESPERSON: May I help you?

FERNANDO: I want some sneakers for my sister. She likes red.

CHORUS: *Silvia likes red. She wants some sneakers.*

◊   ◊   ◊

SALESPERSON: Here are some sneakers. They have red shoelaces.

FERNANDO: I like those shoes.

CHORUS   SALESPERSON   MYRA   FERNANDO

MYRA: Look! Here are some red boots. I like these boots.

FERNANDO: Silvia wants sneakers. What else do you see?

SALESPERSON: Here are some sneakers. They have blue stripes.

FERNANDO: Silvia likes stripes.

CHORUS: *Silvia likes stripes. She likes red. Which sneakers does Fernando like?*

◊ ◊ ◊

MYRA: Which sneakers do you like?

FERNANDO: I like those sneakers. I want the sneakers with red shoelaces. Silvia will like them.

SALESPERSON: What shoe size do you need?

FERNANDO: Oh, no! I don't know Silvia's shoe size!

CHORUS: *Fernando doesn't know Silvia's shoe size. Oh, no!*

MYRA: That's OK, Fernando. Silvia and I wear the same size!

267

Try Out Language

Listen and Chant

WHAT will I WEAR?

It's sunny today.
What will I wear?
I'll wear these sandals
And the T-shirt over there.

Make your own chant.

gloves

windy

jacket

coat

snowy

boots

Vocabulary

Describing Words

🎧 Listen to your teacher.

Use these words to describe the weather.

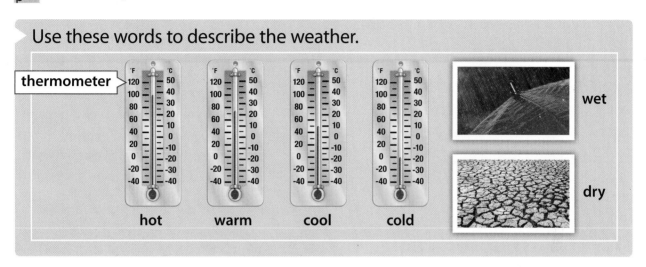

thermometer

hot warm cool cold

wet

dry

🎧 Listen to your teacher. 💬 Talk about the weather in the picture. Say each sentence.

1

It's warm and dry today.

3

It's cool and wet today.

2

It's cold today.

Describe the Weather

💬 Work with a partner. Point to a picture. Your partner describes the weather.

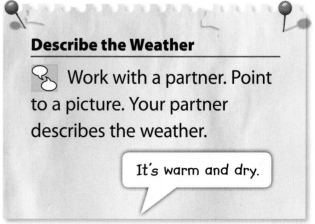

It's warm and dry.

269

Vocabulary

Weather and Describing Words

👓 Look at the weather forecast.

👂 Listen to your teacher.

💬 Describe the weather on each day.

KEY WORDS

cloudy	rainy
cold	snowy
cool	sunny
foggy	warm
hot	windy

Sunday

windy

cool

It's windy and cool today.

Monday

sunny

hot

It's sunny and hot today.

Tuesday	Wednesday	Thursday	Friday	Saturday
rainy	cloudy	foggy	rainy	snowy
warm	warm	cool	cool	cold
It's rainy and warm today.	It's cloudy and warm today.	It's foggy and cool today.	It's rainy and cool today.	It's snowy and cold today.

Talk About the Weather

Work with a partner. Choose a day. Describe the weather to your partner. Take turns.

Express Ideas

Listen and Say

Use sentences like these to tell what you need, want, or have to do.

It's _____ today. I need to _____ .	It's _____ today. I want to _____ .	It's _____ today. I have to _____ .

It's Cold and Snowy

Celia: It's cold and snowy today. I want to walk in the snow.

Yolanda: Great idea! But I need to find my boots. Where are they?

Celia: They're in the closet. I want to wear my warm coat.

Yolanda: I will wear my warm coat, too.

Celia: I have to wear a scarf.

Yolanda: Don't forget your hat and mittens!

Celia: OK. Let's go!

How It Works

Use **it's** with weather words and time and day words.

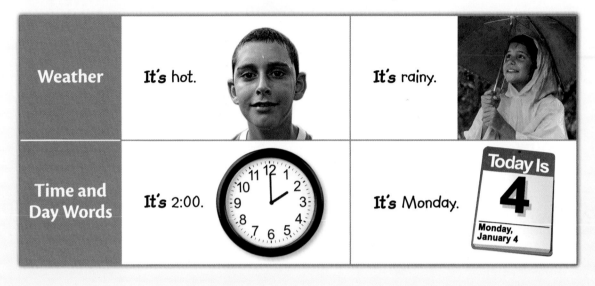

Weather	It's hot.		It's rainy.
Time and Day Words	It's 2:00.		It's Monday.

Talk Together

 Work with a partner. Use your pictures. Tell what the weather is like in each picture. Talk about what you want, need, or have to wear.

Word File Pictures
NGReach.com

It's sunny today. I want to wear shorts.

273

High Frequency Words

Review

Read each word aloud. Use the correct word in each sentence.

has	your
have	help
with	how

1 I need _____ help.

2 Can you _____ us?

3 Yes. I can come _____ my friends.

Learn New Words

Listen to your teacher. Say each new word.

4 **need**
We **need** to put things in boxes.

5 **little**
We have big and **little** boxes.

6 **them**
We will put **them** on a truck.

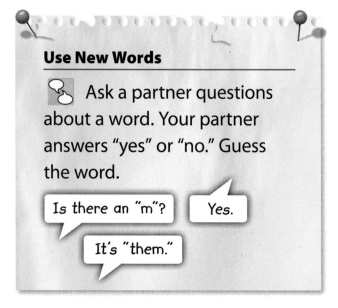

Use New Words

Ask a partner questions about a word. Your partner answers "yes" or "no." Guess the word.

Is there an "m"?

Yes.

It's "them."

PEG AND MEG

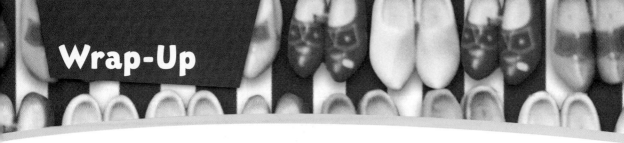

Wrap-Up

Listen and Read Along

 Think about what the book is about.

ANN MORRIS

SHOES
SHOES
SHOES

CD 3
Track 22 (((MP3)))

sandals

shoes

sneakers

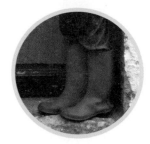

boots

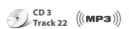

Talk About It

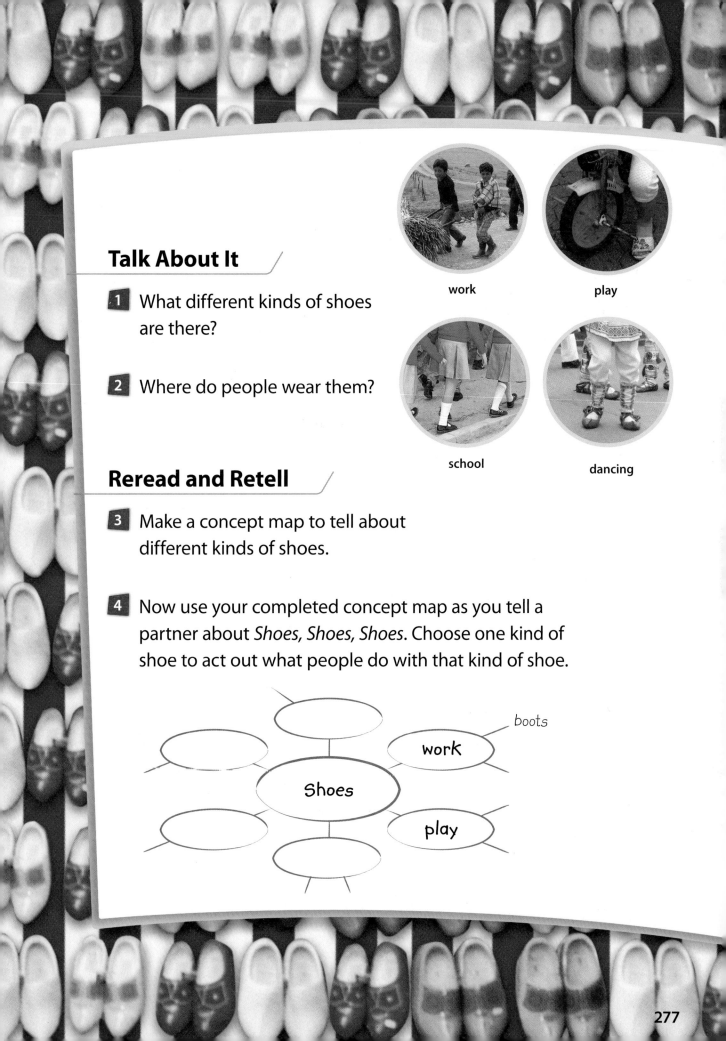

work

play

1 What different kinds of shoes are there?

2 Where do people wear them?

school

dancing

Reread and Retell

3 Make a concept map to tell about different kinds of shoes.

4 Now use your completed concept map as you tell a partner about *Shoes, Shoes, Shoes*. Choose one kind of shoe to act out what people do with that kind of shoe.

boots

work

Shoes

play

Write a Letter and a List

Learn About Sentences

A **statement** tells something. It ends with a **period**.

I am cold. ◁ period

A sentence that shows strong feeling is called an **exclamation**. It ends with an **exclamation point**.

It's really cold here! ◁ exclamation point

✍ Copy each sentence. Add a period or an exclamation point.

1 It's really hot today

2 I want to wear sandals

3 It is rainy outside

4 The wind is really cold

5 It is windy today

6 It is sunny today

February 10

Dear Hala,

I'm glad you are coming to Michigan soon. It's really cold here! Here is what you need to bring:

coat
gloves
hat
scarf

I can't wait to see you.

Your friend,
Noura

Write

Now write a letter to your friend. Your friend is coming to visit you. Tell about the weather. Tell what clothes your friend needs to bring for the weather.

Check Your Writing

Read your work to a partner. Check the writing. Do you need to add a period or an exclamation point at the end of a sentence?

Unit 9

Around Town

In This Unit

▶ **Language:** Give Directions; Express Intentions; Describe Actions

▶ **Vocabulary:** Community Places and Workers; Location Words; Products; Plurals; Vehicles; Words for People

▶ **Reading:** Learn High Frequency Words; Learn Letters and Sounds *Zz, Yy, Ququ, Xx, Uu*; Decode and Spell words with Short *u*; Summarize *Get Around in the City*

▶ **Writing:** Use Adjectives and Nouns; Write Sentences

Unit Project

COMMUNITY MAP

1. List places in your community.
2. Draw a map.
3. Label your map.
4. Use the map to talk about the places.

> The school is next to the fire station.

Listen and Chant

Walk
in the Community

Walk in the community.

Watch the people work.

Walk in the community.

Talk to a clerk.

Talk to a dentist

And a firefighter , too.

Talk to a doctor .

They are here to help you.

Make your own chant.

teller

police officer

cashier

mechanic

Vocabulary

Community Workers

 Look at each picture.

 Listen to your teacher.

 Say the name of each worker.

1

cashier

5

firefighter

8

police officer

2

clerk

6

instructor

9

teller

3
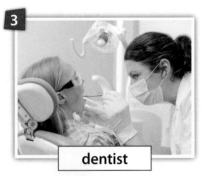
dentist

7

mechanic

10

waiter

4

doctor / nurse

Name Community Workers

Name a community worker. Your partner points to the picture.

Vocabulary

Community Places

👂 Listen to your teacher.

💬 Say the name of each community place.

KEY WORDS

bank
community youth center
dentist's office
fire station
gas station

hospital
police station
post office
restaurant
supermarket

Talk About Your Community

💬 Work with a partner. Use your pictures. Tell where each community worker works.

The _____ works in the _____ .

cashier

supermarket

Word File Pictures
🌐 NGReach.com

284

Vocabulary

Location Words

Listen to your teacher.

Say where the place are.

1

The police station is **on** Main Street.

4

The dentist's office is **above** the bank.

7

The police station is **on the left**.

2

The gas station is **next to** the police station.

5

The bank is **below** the dentist's office.

8

The fire station is **on the right**.

3

The police station is **between** the gas station and the fire station.

6

The hospital is **across from** the restaurant.

Use Location Words

Draw a simple map of places in your community. Label the places. Work with a partner. Tell your partner where the places are.

> The restaurant is next to the bank.

285

Give Directions

CD 4 Track 2 ((MP3))

Listen and Say

Use sentences like these to tell someone how to go to a place.

QUESTION	ANSWERS	
Where is the _____ ?	Go _____ .	The _____ is on _____ .
	Turn left at _____ .	It is _____ .
	Turn right at _____ .	The _____ is _____ the _____ .

Where Is the Post Office?

Scott: Excuse me. Where is the post office?

Jenny: Go down Main Street. Go one block. Turn left at the corner. Then turn right at First Street.

Scott: First Street?

Jenny: Yes. The post office is on First Street. It is next to the bank.

Scott: Thank you!

Jenny: You're welcome.

Use the Right Word

Use **at** or **on** to tell where a place is.

at	on
Use **at** if you know the exact address or place. The post office is **at** 17 First Street. Turn left **at** the corner.	Use **on** if you know just the street name in the address. The post office is **on** First Street.

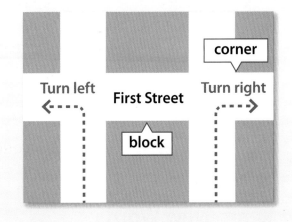

Talk Together

Work with a partner. Look at the map on page 284. Ask your partner where a place is. Your partner tells you how to get there.

Where is the dentist's office?

Go up First Avenue. Turn right at Main Street. The dentist's office is between the restaurant and the supermarket.

High Frequency Words

Review

 Read each word aloud. Use the correct word in each sentence.

is	are

with	need

them	these

1 The post office _____ across the street.

2 What do you _____ ?

3 I need to mail _____ letters.

Learn New Words

 Listen to your teacher. Say each new word.

4 **on**
I live **on** Second Street.

5 **Where**
Where do you live?

6 **around**
I live **around** the corner, on Fifth Avenue.

Use New Words

Say a sentence with a blank for a new word. Your partner says the sentence with the new word.

> I live ___ Main Street.

> I live on Main Street.

Letters and Sounds

Listen and Say

👂 Listen to your teacher. 💬 Say the name of each picture. Say the first sound.

Zz　　**Yy**　　**Uu**　　**Qu qu**　　**Xx**

👂 Listen to each word. What letter spells the <u>first</u> sound you hear?

👂 Listen to each word. What letters spell the <u>first</u> <u>two</u> sounds you hear?

👂 Listen to each word. What letters spell the <u>last</u> <u>two</u> sounds you hear?

Wrap-Up

Play a Game

How to Play

1. Play with two other players.

2. Player 1 chooses a place on the map. He or she asks for directions.

> Where is the post office?

3. Player 2 gives directions from the star ⭐ to the place. Player 1 traces the directions on the board with a finger.

> Go down Seventh Street.
> Turn right on West Street.
> The post office is at 72 West Street.

4. If the directions are correct, Player 2 gets a point.

5. Then Player 2 asks for directions to a place. Player 3 gives directions.

6. The player with the most points wins.

Post Office
72 West Street

West Street

290

Dentist's Office
126 Eighth Street

Gas Station
108 Eighth Street

Eighth Street

Where Is the Post Office?

Police Station
105 Eighth Street

Hospital
76 Town Street

Seventh Street

Community Youth Center
62 Town Street

Town Street

Bank
64 Lake Street

Supermarket
60 Lake Street

Lake Street

Fire Station
110 Sixth Street

Sixth Street

Restaurant
119 Sixth Street

Going Shopping

I am going to buy some books.

I am going to buy some fruit.

I am going to buy some flowers.

I am going to buy some shoes.

I am going to buy some tickets.

I am going to buy some combs.

And when I finish shopping,

I am going to go home.

fruit

flowers

tickets

292

Vocabulary

Products

 Listen to your teacher.

| one | more than one |

The name for more than one thing often ends in **-s**.

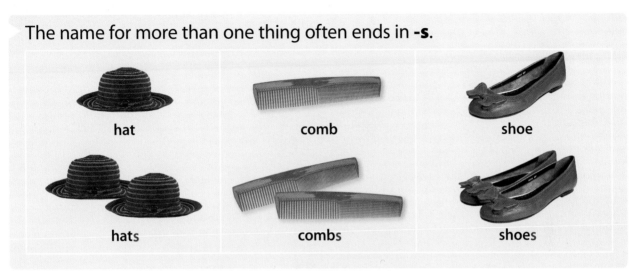

| hat | comb | shoe |
| hats | combs | shoes |

👓 Look at the picture. 👂 Listen to your teacher.

💬 Say the word for each item. Add *-s* for more than one.

jacket

sweater

shirt

skirt

clothing store

Tell What You Can Buy

👥 Work with a partner. Tell what you can buy at a clothing store. Add *-s* for more than one.

I can buy some _____ at a clothing store.

Vocabulary

Community Places and Products

Listen to your teacher.

Say the name of each place and each product.

1

flower shop

3

bookstore

2

movie theater

4

shoe store

294

5

apples

fruit stand

8

hammers

hardware store

6

combs

hair salon

9

thermometers

pharmacy

7

caps

clothing store

10

baskets

laundromat

Talk About What You Can Buy

🗨 Work with a partner. Tell what you can buy in different stores.

I can buy some _____ at a _____ .

295

Express Intentions

Listen and Say

Use sentences like these to tell what you plan to do.

I am going to _____ .	I will _____ .

This Weekend

Julie: What are you going to do on Saturday?

Cristina: I am going to buy some flowers at the flower shop. I will give them to my mom.

Julie: What else are you going to do?

Cristina: Then I am going to buy some shoes at the shoe store.

Julie: You are so busy!

Cristina: What are you going to do this weekend?

Julie: I am going to act in a play. I will sing a song, too. Come and see me!

Cristina: Good idea! I will.

How It Works

Listen to these words. Listen for the **-s** at the end of each word. It means more than one. Now say the words with a partner. Be sure to say the **-s** at the end of each word.

basket**s**	apple**s**
book**s**	comb**s**
cap**s**	flower**s**
sock**s**	hammer**s**
ticket**s**	shoe**s**

Talk Together

Work with a partner. Use your pictures. Tell what you are going to buy at each place. Use *I am going to* or *I will*.

Word File Pictures
⊘ NGReach.com

> I am going to buy some caps at the clothing store.

297

High Frequency Words

Review

🗨 Read each word aloud. Use the correct word in each sentence.

at	on

1 I live _____ Main Street.

Who	Where

2 _____ do you live?

around	are

3 I live _____ the corner.

Learn New Words

👂 Listen to your teacher. 🗨 Say each new word.

4 **work**
I **work** at the library after school.

5 **take**
I **take** a snack with me.

6 **give**
My mom will **give** me a ride.

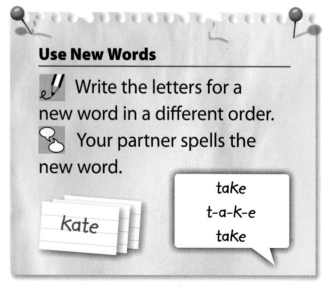

Use New Words

✏ Write the letters for a new word in a different order.
🗨 Your partner spells the new word.

Kate

take
t-a-k-e
take

Letters and Sounds

Read a Word

💬 Blend the sounds to read a word.

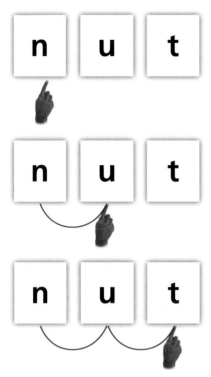

u

n
nʊ
nʊt

Read More Words

💬 Read the words to a partner.

1 cut

2 nut

3 bus

4 cup

5 pup

6 sun

7 fun

8 bun

9 yum

Make New Words

🖊 Use these letters. Write words on cards. ✌ Practice reading with a partner.

y	c	n	b
m	p	s	f	u

pup

CD 4
Track 6 (((MP3)))

Theme Theater

Yolanda and Oscar are going into town. They have many
things to do. Listen to their conversation. Then act it out.

A Day in Town

OSCAR: What are you doing today, Yolanda?

YOLANDA: I am going to town.

OSCAR: What are you going to do?

YOLANDA: First, I am going to the post office.
Then, I'm going shopping.

OSCAR: Can I come with you? I need
to go to the library. I need to get
a book for school.

YOLANDA: Yes, we can go to town together.

CHORUS: *Oscar and Yolanda are going to town.*
They have much to do.

◇   ◇   ◇

YOLANDA: First, I will mail these letters.

OSCAR: OK. The fruit stand is on the corner.
I am hungry. I am going to buy some
apples. Meet me there.

YOLANDA: OK. See you at the corner.

CLERK: Can I help you?

YOLANDA: I want to mail these letters.

CLERK: That will be four dollars and twenty cents.

YOLANDA: Here you are.

CHORUS: *Oscar and Yolanda will meet at the corner.*

OSCAR: What are you going to do now?

YOLANDA: Now I am going to buy some combs at the hair salon.

OSCAR: I am going to the clothing store. I will buy a cap.

YOLANDA: Then we can see a movie.

OSCAR: Good idea. I will meet you at the movie theater. Then we will go to the library.

CHORUS: *Yolanda and Oscar will see a movie. Then they will go to the library.*

◊   ◊   ◊

OSCAR: That was a long movie. What time is it? I still need that book!

YOLANDA: There is the library.

OSCAR: Oh, no! The library is closed! I can't get the book!

YOLANDA: I feel bad! What will you do?

OSCAR: I will get it tomorrow.

YOLANDA: Good idea!

Go Downtown

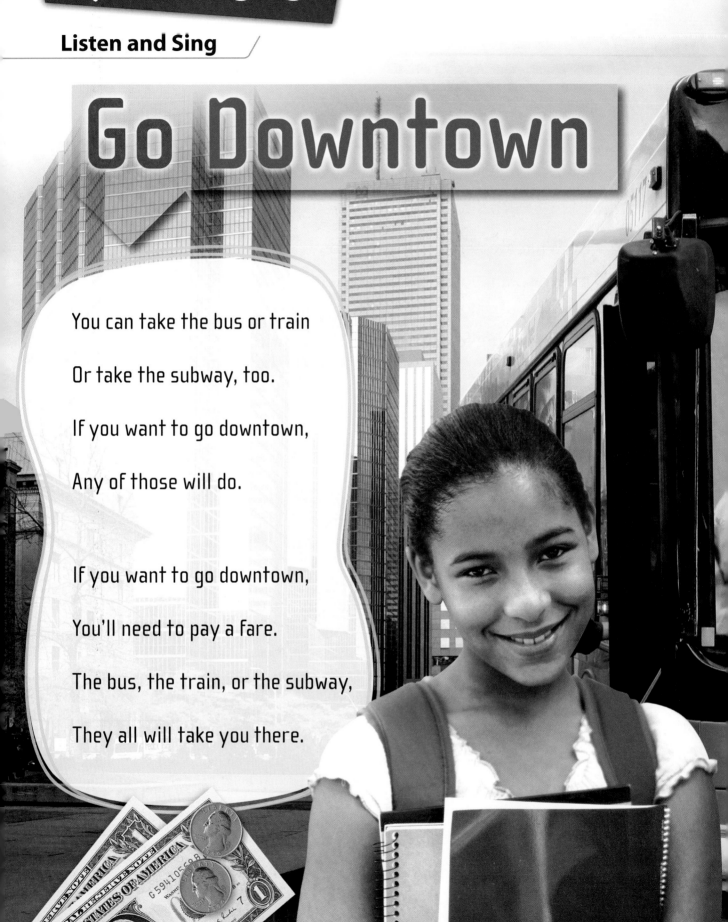

You can take the bus or train

Or take the subway, too.

If you want to go downtown,

Any of those will do.

If you want to go downtown,

You'll need to pay a fare.

The bus, the train, or the subway,

They all will take you there.

Vehicles

👓 Look at each picture.

👂 Listen to your teacher.

🗨 Say the name of each vehicle.

1 bicycle

2 bus

3 car

4 train

5 skateboard

Name Vehicles

🗨 Point to a vehicle. Your partner names the vehicle and tells something about it.

> Bus. It is big. It is blue and white.

More Vehicles

👓 Look at each picture.

👂 Listen to your teacher.

🗨 Say the name of each vehicle.

6 airplane

7 ambulance

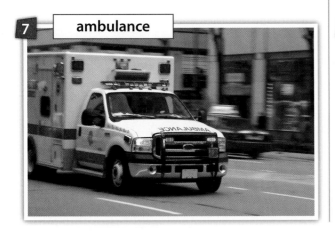

8 motorcycle

9 subway

10 taxi

Name Vehicles

🗨 Point to a vehicle. Your partner names the vehicle and tells something about it.

> Subway. It is long.

Words for People

 Listen to your teacher.

> When you talk about more than one person, use **they**.
> When you tell about what they own, use **their**.
>
> My friends like to go places. **They** go everywhere.
> They ride **their** bikes all day long.

 Listen to your teacher.   Say the sentences.

1

The students ride on their skateboards. They wear helmets.

2

The people drive their cars to work. They do not want to be late.

3

My parents like to ride their motorcycles. They go to visit family and friends.

Talk About Your Friends

Work with a partner. Tell how your friends go places. Talk about the vehicles they use.

> My friends ride their bicycles. They ride to school. Their bicycles are new.

Describe Actions

Listen and Say

Use sentences like these to tell how people go places.

| They ride _____ . | They ride on a _____ .
They ride in a _____ . | They take _____ . |

1

People go everywhere! They ride bicycles. They ride motorcycles.

2

They ride on a train.

3

They ride in a car.

4

They take the bus or the subway.
They also take a taxi.

306

Use the Right Word

Use **in** or **on** when you talk about riding vehicles.

in	on	
Use **in** with these vehicles.	Use **on** with these vehicles.	
They ride **in** a car.	I ride **on** a skateboard.	We ride **on** a bus.
I ride **in** an ambulance.	I ride **on** a bicycle.	They ride **on** a train.
We ride **in** a taxi.	They ride **on** a motorcycle.	I ride **on** the subway.
They ride **in** an airplane.		

Talk Together

Work with a partner. Talk about the vehicles on your picture cards. Use each picture. Make a sentence with *they ride* or *they take*.

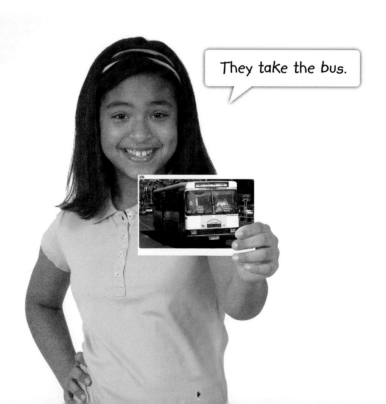

They take the bus.

High Frequency Words

Review

 Read each word aloud. Use the correct word in each sentence.

has	have

1 Will you _____ a party?

answer	need

2 I asked my parents, but they didn't _____ me.

they	them

3 Ask _____ again.

Learn New Words

 Listen to your teacher.   Say each new word.

4 **to**
I am going **to** study for our history test.

5 **which**
Which dates do we need to know?

6 **here**
Look **here**, in your notebook.

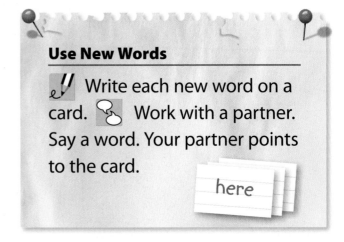

Use New Words

Write each new word on a card.   Work with a partner. Say a word. Your partner points to the card.

here

308

Letters and Sounds

Spell and Read

Look at the picture. Use your letter cards to spell the word.

Then read the word.

1

r __ __

2

f __ __

3

s __ __

4
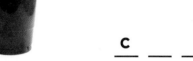

c __ __

5

p __ __

sun
s–u–n
sun

Spell More Words

Work with a partner. Use your letter cards to spell words.

r f s c p n u

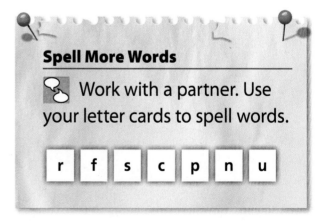

Listen and Read Along

Think about what the book is about.
Which vehicles do you know?

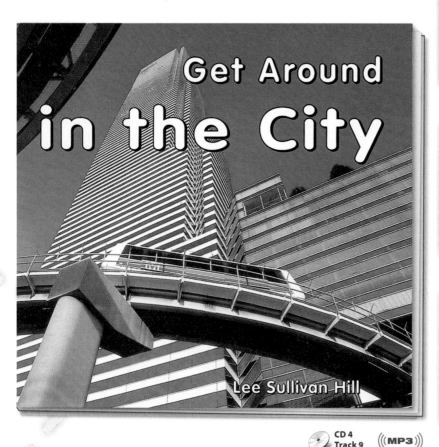

Get Around
in the City

Lee Sullivan Hill

CD 4
Track 9 (((MP3)))

rickshaw

bus

ferry

cart

Talk About It

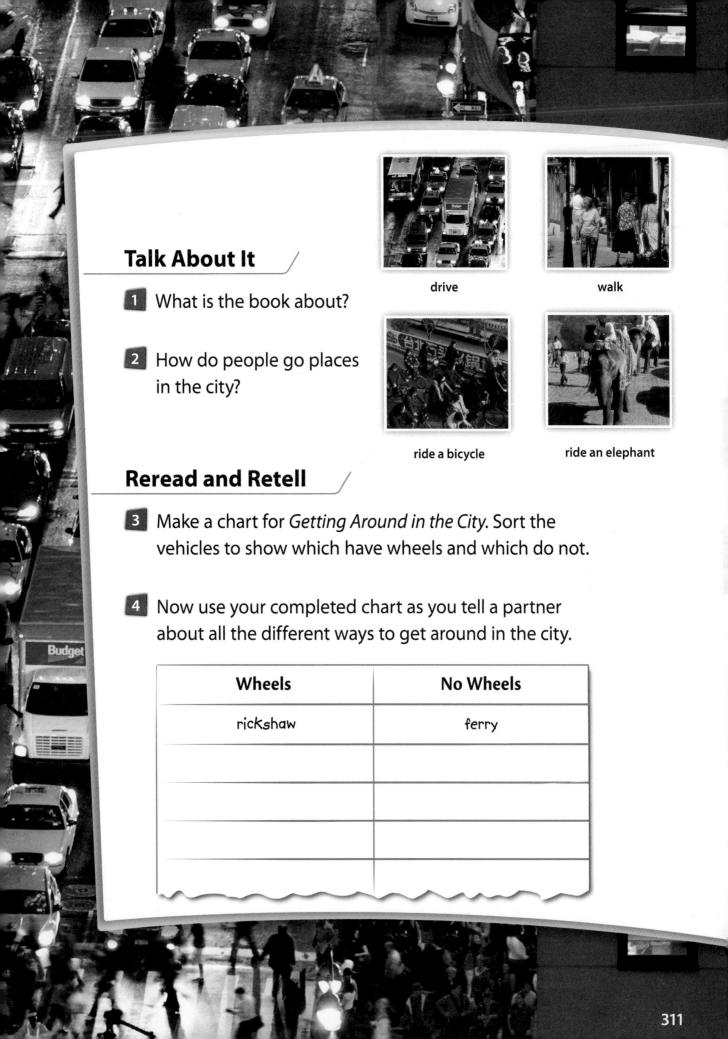

1. What is the book about?

2. How do people go places in the city?

drive

walk

ride a bicycle

ride an elephant

Reread and Retell

3. Make a chart for *Getting Around in the City*. Sort the vehicles to show which have wheels and which do not.

4. Now use your completed chart as you tell a partner about all the different ways to get around in the city.

Wheels	No Wheels
rickshaw	ferry

Write About Your Favorite Place

Learn About Nouns

A **noun** names a person, place, animal, or thing. Nouns add details to sentences. You can put **describing words** before nouns.

He is a math tutor.

describing word   noun

Describing Words	Nouns
big	day
First	map
green	notebook
long	Street
rainy	teacher
science	train

Copy each sentence. Add a describing word and a noun that finish the sentence. Use the words in the chart.

1. Today is a _____ _____.

2. I have a _____ _____.

3. He is a _____ _____.

4. Look at the _____ _____ on the wall.

5. They ride on a _____ _____.

6. Turn left at _____ _____.

Study a Model

OAKVILLE YOUTH CENTER
I like the Oakville Youth Center. It is my favorite place.

I see Mr. Jones. He is a math tutor.

I talk with Eduardo. He is a good friend.

I take a picture with a camera.

Write

Now write about your favorite place. Draw pictures or tape photos of people and activities at your favorite place.

Check Your Writing

Read your work to a partner. Check the writing. Do you have nouns and describing words? Are your words in the right order?

Unit 10

All Year Long

In This Unit

▶ **Language:** Describe Actions; Make a Request

▶ **Vocabulary:** Seasons and Activities; Months; Dates; Making Things; Celebrations; Review Pronouns

▶ **Reading:** Learn High Frequency Words; Read Decodable Text; Explain *Weather and Seasons*

▶ **Writing:** Subject-Verb Agreement; Write Sentences

Unit Project

YEARBOOK

1. Work with a group. Focus on one month of the year.

2. Brainstorm activities. Make a page.

3. Organize the pages.

4. Present your page. Listen to other groups.

In April, we plant seeds.

Listen and Sing

Every Season of the Year

fall

Fall and winter, spring and summer,
Every season all year through,
There are lots of things we can do
That are fun for me and you.

winter

In September and October
And November, we have school.
In December, January,
February, snow is cool.

March and April and then May,
It's time to plant flowers again.
Then in June, July, and August,
Summer days should never end.

spring

summer

Fall and winter, spring and summer,
Every season all year through,
There are lots of things we can do
That are fun for me and you.

Seasons and Activities

👂 Listen to your teacher.

🗨 Say the name of each season and activity.

KEY WORDS

winter	sled down a hill
spring	plant seeds
summer	swim in a lake
fall	rake leaves

1 winter

sled down a hill

2 spring

plant seeds

3 summer

swim in a lake

4 fall

rake leaves

Talk About Seasons and Activities

🗨 Talk about your favorite season. Tell what you can do then.

My favorite season is _____. I can _____.

Vocabulary

Months

🦻 Listen to your teacher.

🗨 Say the name of each month.

1 January

2 February

3 March

4 April

5 May

6 June

7 July

8 August

9 September

10 October

11 November

12 December

Talk About Months

🗨 Talk about your favorite month. Tell what you can do then.

My favorite month is _____. I can _____.

318

Vocabulary

Dates

Listen to your teacher.

> When you write or say a date, put the month first.

month	day	year

Write: **January 4, 2011**

↖ Put a comma between the day and the year.

Or write: **1/4/2011**

Say:

> January fourth, two thousand eleven

Listen to your teacher. Say the date that is circled.

1

NOVEMBER 2010

Sunday	Monday	Tuesday	Wednesday	Thursday	Friday	Saturday
	1	2	3	4	5	6
7	8	9	10	11	12	13
14	(15)	16	17	18	19	20
21	22	23	24	25	26	27
28	29	30				

Today is November 15, 2010.

3

SEPTEMBER 2012

Sunday	Monday	Tuesday	Wednesday	Thursday	Friday	Saturday
						1
2	3	4	5	6	7	8
9	10	11	12	13	14	15
16	17	18	19	20	21	22
23	24	25	26	27	(28)	29
30						

Today is September 28, 2012.

2

JULY 2011

Sunday	Monday	Tuesday	Wednesday	Thursday	Friday	Saturday
					(1)	2
3	4	5	6	7	8	9
10	11	12	13	14	15	16
17	18	19	20	21	22	23
24	25	26	27	28	29	30
31						

Today is July 1, 2011.

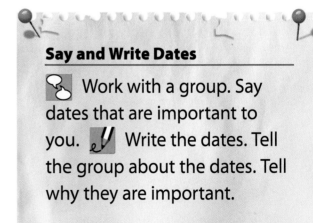

Say and Write Dates

Work with a group. Say dates that are important to you. Write the dates. Tell the group about the dates. Tell why they are important.

Describe Actions

Listen and Say

Use sentences like these to tell what people do in different seasons or months.

In the fall, Tom _____ . In September, he _____ .	In the spring, Malia _____ . In April, she _____ .

What Does Your Family Do?

Juan: Do people in your family do special things every season?

Oscar: Yes. My grandmother likes to bake. In September, she picks apples. Then she makes apple pies. What does your family do?

Juan: My father likes to work in the yard. In the spring, he plants flowers.

Oscar: My mother plants flowers in the spring, too!

How It Works

A **verb** can tell what a person does.

run   write   walk   jump

When you tell what one other person does, add **-s** to the verb.

Kam runs.
Alfredo writes.
She walks.
He jumps.

Talk Together

Work with a partner. Write what you do in each season. Change papers. Then tell the class what your partner does in each season.

In the summer, Leticia runs. In September, she plays soccer.

High Frequency Words

Review

💬 Read each word aloud. Use the correct word in each sentence.

have	has

has	is

her	help

1 I _____ my notebook here.

2 It _____ some answers in it.

3 It will _____ me learn.

Learn New Words

👂 Listen to your teacher.   💬 Say each new word.

4 **in**
I have new words **in** my notebook.

5 **letters**
Every day, I write the **letters** and words I learn.

6 **will**
I **will** write more words tomorrow.

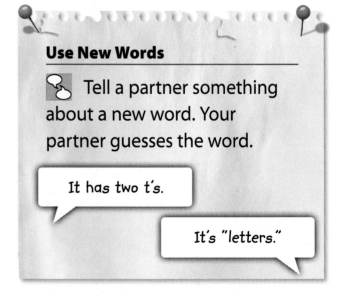

Use New Words

🗣 Tell a partner something about a new word. Your partner guesses the word.

> It has two t's.

> It's "letters."

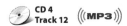
Listen and Chant

 Listen to the chant.   💬 Say the chant with your teacher.

Hot Day, Wet Day

What do you do on a hot, hot day?

We run around.
We sit in the sun.
We dig up yams.
We have some fun.

What do you do on a wet, wet day?

We read a book.
We get on a bus.
We work on the pup
If he got in the mud.

Use Letters and Sounds

💬 How many sounds does each word have? Tell a partner.

| yam | sun | pup |

Play a Game

How to Play

1. Play with a partner.

2. Use a plastic chip.

3. Partner 1 tosses the plastic chip onto the game board to make it land on an activity. Then Partner 1 tells when a family member or a friend does that activity.

   > In the winter, my brother shovels snow.

4. If Partner 1 uses the correct verb with -s, he or she gets a point.

5. Then Partner 2 tosses a plastic chip onto the game board to make it land on an activity.

6. Partners take turns. The winner is the first person to get five points.

Seasons of Fun

play basketball

skate

eat ice cream

shovel snow

pick apples

plant flowers

swim

rake leaves

ride a bicycle

PAPER ART

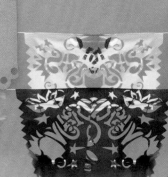

Measure the paper with a ruler.

Fold the paper up just right.

Cut the paper and make a design.

Put it up for the party tonight.

Words for People

 Listen to your teacher.

When you talk about people, use the right word.

he	she	they
Use **he** for one boy or one man.	Use **she** for one girl or one woman.	Use **they** for more than one person.

 Listen to your teacher. Say the sentences.

It's Marc's graduation.
He has a special dinner.

It's Gabriela's graduation.
She wears a pretty dress.

Many people are at the party.
They have fun.

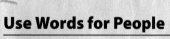

Use Words for People

 Work with a partner. Point to a picture on this page. Say the first sentence. Your partner says the second sentence.

327

Vocabulary

Making Things

🦻 Listen to your teacher.

👓 Look at each picture.

💬 Say the name of each step.

KEY WORDS

greeting card   glue on a picture

measure the paper   write a message

cut the paper   put the card inside

fold the paper   write the address

get the markers   mail the card

Make a greeting card.

Happy Graduation!

1 measure the paper

2 cut the paper

3 fold the paper

328

4 get the markers

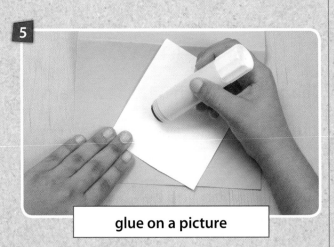

5 glue on a picture

6 write a message

Happy Graduation!

7 put the card inside

ation!

8 write the address

Rita Wong
314 Oak St.
Lakewood, CA

9 mail the card

Lakewood, CA

Tell How to Make a Card

Work with a partner. Talk about the steps in making a greeting card.

Measure the paper.

329

Describe Actions

Listen and Say

Use sentences like these to tell what people do on different holidays.

On New Year's Day, Mom _____ .	On New Year's Day, Dad _____ .	On New Year's Day, my parents _____ .
On New Year's Day, she _____ .	On New Year's Day, he _____ .	On New Year's Day, they _____ .

Chinese New Year

Jean: When is Chinese New Year?

Ling: It's at the end of January or the beginning of February.

Jean: How do you celebrate the New Year?

Ling: My mother cooks a special meal. She makes it the night before. My brother likes to dance. On New Year's Day, he wears a lion costume and dances with a group.

Jean: Do *you* do anything special?

Ling: I visit my grandparents. They give me money in red envelopes!

How It Works

A **verb** can tell what a person does.	When you tell what one other person does, add **-s** to the verb.	When you tell what two or more people do, do not change anything.
cook	My aunt cooks.	My parents cook.
swim	She swims.	They swim.
play	My friend plays soccer.	My friends play soccer.
write	He writes stories.	They write stories.

Talk Together

Work with a partner. Tell what you do on different holidays. Then work with a group. Tell the group what your partner does on different holidays.

On New Year's Day, he eats special food.

High Frequency Words

Review

🗨 Read each word aloud. Use the correct word in each sentence.

Tomorrow	**Day**

1 _____ is the last day of school!

is	**will**

2 What _____ you do this summer?

help	**give**

3 I will _____ my mother at the store.

Learn New Words

👂 Listen to your teacher. 🗨 Say each new word.

4 **night**
In the winter, **night** comes early.

5 **think**
Yes, I **think** summer is better.

6 **later**
I like it when night comes **later**.

7 **for**
Summer is better **for** baseball.

Use New Words

✍ Write the letters for a new word in a different order.
🗨 Your partner spells the new word.

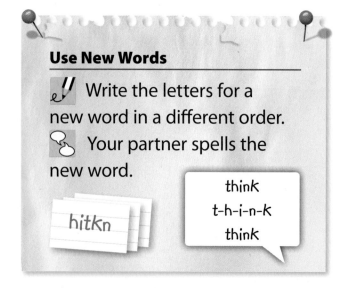

think
t-h-i-n-k
think

hitkn

332

SUMMER FUN

NAN HAS FUN WITH HER PUP, BUD.

BUD SEES A BUG. HE JUMPS.

BUD SEES A BUS. HE RUNS.

NAN AND BUD RUN UP THE HILL.

NAN HUGS BUD AS THE SUN SETS.

NAN HAS A HOT DOG IN A BUN.

It is not for you.

THEN THEY REST ON A RUG.

Theme Theater

It is Kim's graduation day. Kim and her brother Loc are telling Leila about her party. Listen to their conversation. Then act it out.

The Party Problem

LEILA: Congratulations, Kim! I made you a card.

KIM: Thank you.

LEILA: Will you have a graduation party?

KIM: Yes. We will have a party on Saturday.

LOC: It will be a family party only.

KIM: I want to have some friends at my party. But my mom says that will be too many people.

LOC: Our family is big!

CHORUS: *It is Kim's graduation day. She wants to have some friends at her party.*

◊   ◊   ◊

LEILA: What do your parents usually do for a party?

KIM: My mom cooks special food. She is a great cook.

LEILA: What does your dad do?

KIM: My dad makes a cake. He decorates it with many colors.

CHORUS: *Kim's mom cooks for a party. Kim's dad bakes a cake.*

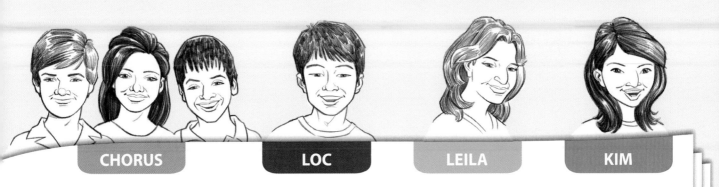

LEILA: I think your party will be fun.

KIM: I want you to come to my party.
I will ask my parents tonight.

LEILA: OK. See you tomorrow,
Kim. Bye, Loc.

KIM: See you later, Leila.

LOC: Bye, Leila.

◊ ◊ ◊

LOC: Surprise!

CHORUS: *Surprise!*

KIM: What is happening?
All my friends are here.

LOC: It is a surprise party! Our family is here.
All your friends are here, too.

LEILA: Loc talked to your mom and dad.
He told them you wanted to have friends
at your graduation party.

KIM: Thanks, everyone. I'm so happy!

CHORUS: *Kim is happy. All her friends are at the party.*

Listen and Chant

How You Celebrate

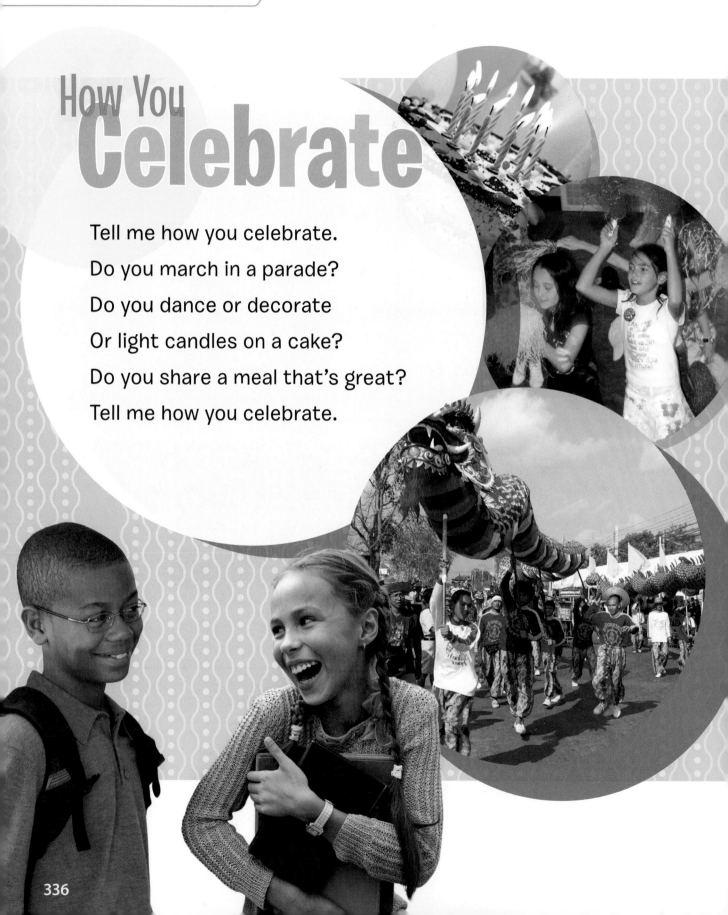

Tell me how you celebrate.

Do you march in a parade?

Do you dance or decorate

Or light candles on a cake?

Do you share a meal that's great?

Tell me how you celebrate.

Vocabulary

Words for People

Listen to your teacher.

When you talk about people, use the right word.

I	you	we
Use **I** to talk about yourself.	Use **you** to talk to another person.	Use **we** to talk about yourself and another person.

Listen to your teacher. Say each sentence.

1

I wear special clothes.

3

We dance together.

2

You play music.

Use Words for People

Work with a partner. Tell your partner what you and your family do to celebrate special days.

I send cards.

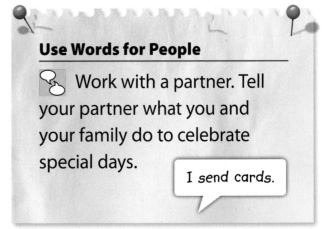

Vocabulary

Celebrations

🦻 Listen to your teacher.

💬 Say the name of each activity.

3 light candles

1 dance together

4 make a cake

2 decorate our home

5 march in a parade

6

open a gift

7

send a card

8

share a meal

9

wear special clothes

10

wrap a present

Use Words for Celebrations

Work with a partner. Talk about your favorite activity during a celebration.

My favorite activity is _____.

339

Make a Request

Listen and Say

Use a question like this to ask someone to do something.

QUESTION	ANSWER
Will you please _____ ?	Sure.

Use questions like these to ask for something you want.

QUESTIONS		ANSWER
May I _____ ?	May we _____ ?	Of course.

The Cinco de Mayo Party

Arturo: Tomorrow is Cinco de Mayo. That's May 5. Are you coming to my party?

Miguel: Yes! I am excited about it.

Arturo: I need to decorate our home. Will you please help me?

Miguel: Sure. May I bring my cousin to the party? She is visiting from Mexico.

Arturo: Of course.

Miguel: May we bring some music?

Arturo: That will be great.

Miguel: See you tomorrow.

Arturo: Bye!

Use the Right Word

Use polite words for different reasons.

Excuse me.	May I please . . .	Will you please . . .
Use **Excuse me** to get someone's attention. **Excuse me.** Do you have the time?	Use **May I please** to ask if you can do something. **May I please** use your calculator?	Use **Will you please** to ask someone to do something for you. **Will you please** help me?

Talk Together

Work with a partner. Take turns making requests about celebrations.

Will you please make a cake?

Sure.

High Frequency Words

Review

Read each word aloud. Use the correct word in each sentence.

think	look

am	are

Who	What

1 I _____ summer is better than winter.

2 The days _____ long.

3 _____ do you think?

Learn New Words

Listen to your teacher. Say each new word.

4 **see**
In the summer, you don't need lights to $\boxed{\text{see}}$ the ball.

5 **soon**
It will be summer $\boxed{\text{soon}}$.
I can't wait!

6 **year**
It is the best time of the $\boxed{\text{year}}$!

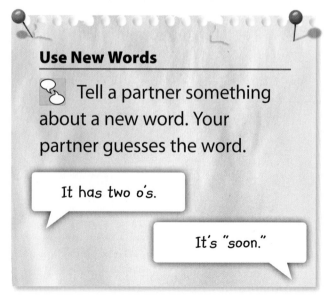

Use New Words

Tell a partner something about a new word. Your partner guesses the word.

It has two o's.

It's "soon."

WHEN CAN I HAVE FUN?

I LUG THE JUG. I DO NOT RUN.

I CUT THE BUNS.

I HUM AND MOP UP THE MUD.

I SET THE CUPS AND MUGS IN THE SUDS.

THEN, I GET ON THE BUS.

NOW I GET TO HAVE FUN!

Listen and Read Along

 Think about what the book is about.

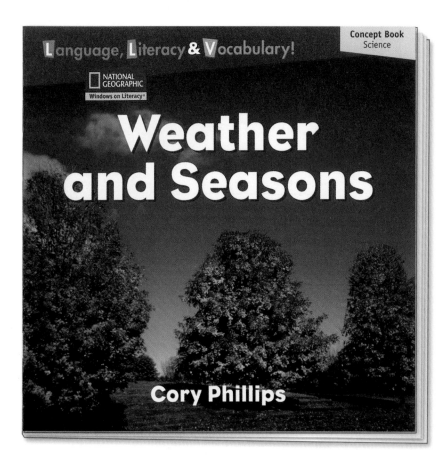

Language, Literacy & Vocabulary!

Concept Book
Science

NATIONAL GEOGRAPHIC
Windows on Literacy®

Weather and Seasons

Cory Phillips

 CD 4 Track 18 (((MP3)))

spring

summer

fall

winter

Talk About It

rainy

windy

1. What is the book about?

2. What do people do on different kinds of days?

sunny

snowy

Reread and Retell

3. Make two diagrams to tell about the main ideas of *Weather and Seasons*. Add details to each one.

4. Now use your completed main idea diagrams as you tell a partner about *Weather and Seasons*.

Season	Weather
spring	rainy, windy

Weather	Activity
windy	fly a kite

Write About a Celebration

Learn About Verbs

A **verb** can tell what someone or something does.

I	
We	
You	**make** cards.
They	

Add **-s** to the verb with **he**, **she**, and **it**.

He	
She	**makes** special food.
It	**makes** noise.

 Copy each sentence. Write the verb correctly.

1 We _____ cards for Valentine's Day. (make)

2 They _____ a meal on Thanksgiving. (share)

3 She _____ gifts in pretty paper. (wrap)

4 You _____ your home. (decorate)

5 He _____ special clothes for New Year's Day. (wear)

6 I _____ gifts on my birthday. (open)

Tet – The Vietnamese New Year
by Trong Pham

In January or February, we celebrate Tet. For Tet, we do special things.

My father makes
special food.

We decorate our home
with flowers.

Write

Now write about your favorite celebration.
Draw pictures or tape photos to your page.

Check Your Writing

Read your work to a partner. Check the writing.
Are your verbs correct? Do you have -s at the end of
verbs for *he*, *she*, or *it*?

Index

a
b
c
d
e
f
g
h
i
j
k
l
m
n
o
p
q
r
s
t
u
v
w
x
y
z

Acknowledgments, continued

Illustrator Credits

270-271 (weather icons) Ken Batelman. **75** Pamela Becker. **323** Chi Chung. **246** Cheryl Cook. **157, 255** Dartmouth Publishing. **310-311** Illustrations from *Get Around in the City* by Lee Sullivan Hill. Copyright © by Lee Sullivan Hill. Used by permission of Carolrhoda Books, Inc., a division of Lerner Publishing Group. All rights reserved. **209** Eric Hoffsten. **22-23, 58-59, 90-91, 130-131, 164-165, 196-197, 232-233, 266-267, 300-301, 334-335** Cedric Hohnstadt Illustration. **40-41, 52-53, 180-181, 247, 248** Terry Julien. **32-33** Illustrations from *From Here to* There by Marjorie Cuyler. Text copyright © 1999 by Margery Cuyler. Illustrations © 1999 by Yu Cha Pak. Used courtesy of Henry Holt and Company. **284-285** Jun Park. 185 Karen Prichett. **57, 67, 129, 141, 195, 205, 265, 275, 333, 343** Ben Shannon. **253** James Yamasaki.

Photographic Credits

iv: (tl) © Image copyright michaeljung, 2009. Used under license from Shutterstock.com. **iv:** (t) Thinkstock Images/Comstock/Jupiter Images. **iv:** (tr) Hill Street Studios/Blend Images/Getty Images. **iv:** (bl) ©NGSP. **v:** (tl) Masterfile (Royalty-Free Div.). **v:** (t) ©Suto Norbert/Fotolia. **v:** (tr) © Rob/Fotolia. **v:** (l) ©Getty Images. **v:** (l) © devon. Image from BigStockPhoto.com. **v:** (l) ©Getty Images. **v:** (l) ©Superstock. **v:** (l) ©NGSP. **v:** (l) ©Metatools. **v:** (l) ©Artville. **v:** (l) Photodisc/Alamy. **v:** (l) 2008 © Robyn Mackenzie. Image from BigStockPhoto .com. **v:** (l) ©Getty Images. **v:** (bl) ©NGSP. **vi:** (tl) © Masterfile / Radius Images/Jupiter Images. **vi:** (t) © Image copyright David Dohnal, 2009. Used under license from Shutterstock.com. **vi:** (tr) Terry Vine/Blend Images/Getty Images. **vi:** (bl) ©NGSP. **vii:** (tl) John Lund/ Drew Kelly/Jupiter Images. **vii:** (t) © 2008, Hathaway/ Big Stock Photo. **vii:** (tr) © Jake Hellbach / Alamy. **vii:** (bl) ©NGSP. **viii:** (tl) ©Jupiter Images. **viii:** (t) Masterfile (Royalty-Free Div.). **vii:** (tr) ©Artville. **viii:** (bl) ©NGSP. **ix:** (tl) Hill Street/Jupiter Images. **ix:** (tr) John Burcham/ Getty Images. **ix:** (tr) © B.A.E. Inc. / Alamy. **ix:** (bl) ©NGSP. **x:** (tl) Barbara Penoyar/Jupiter Images. **x:** (t) © Sonyae | Dreamstime.com. **x:** (tr) bilderlounge/ bilderlounge/Jupiter Images. **x:** (bl) ©NGSP. **xi:** (tl) Caroline Woodham/Photographer's Choice/Getty Images. **xi:** (tr) fedlog/Big Stock Photo. **xi:** (tr) ©iStockphoto.com/geoarts. **xi:** (l) Stockbyte/Getty Images. **xi:** (bl) ©NGSP. **xii:** (tl) © Valery Shanin/Fotolia. **xi:** (t) © Howard Barlow / Alamy. **xii:** (t) Copyright © Unknown photographer / Photo Edit. **xii:** (bl) ©NGSP. **xiii:** (tl) © Blend Images / Alamy. **xiii:** (t) © Michael Parton / Alamy. **xiii:** (tr) Masterfile (Royalty-Free Div.). **xiii:** (l) ©Ginosphotos | Dreamstime.com. **xiii:** (bl) ©NGSP. **ix:** (t) ©Artville. **2** (c) © William Gutmann/Corbis. (tl) Indeed/Digital Vision/Getty Images. (bl) Hill Street Studios/Blend Images/Getty Images. **3** (tr) Blend Images Photography/Veer. (br) Thinkstock Images/Jupiter Images. **4** (tl) Monartdesign.com/Fotolia. (tr) (C) 2007 Comstock Images/Jupiter Images. (bkgd t) Beth Tenser/ BigStockPhoto. (br) © Monkeybusinessimages/ Dreamstime.com. (bl) Gethin/Fotolia. **5** (c) Alan Marsh/ Getty Images. **6** (bl) Charlene Bayerle/Fotolia. **7** (bl) Chad McDermott/Fotolia. **8** (tl) © Mary Kate Denny/ PhotoEdit. (b) © Image copyright Colour, 2009. Used under license from Shutterstock.com. **9** (b) © amana images inc./Alamy. **10** (cr) John Prescott/iStockphoto. (bl) Joshua Hodge Photography/iStockphoto. **11** (tl) Digital Stock. (cl) Jules Frazier/Photodisc/Getty Images. (bcl) Ryan McVay/Photodisc/Getty Images. (bl) PhotoDisc/Getty Images. (tc) Brand X Pictures/Jupiter Images. (c) Harald Sund/Riser/Getty Images. (bc) Paul Beard/Photodisc/Getty Images. (bc) LWA/Photodisc/ Getty Images. (tr) EyeWire. (cr) Digital Stock. (br) Steve Cole/Photodisc/Getty Images. (br) Metaphotos. (tl) Devonyu/iStockphoto. (tl) C Squared Studios/ Photodisc/Getty Images. (tcl) Digital Stock. (t) Nick Koudis/Photodisc/Getty Images. (tr) PhotoDisc/Getty Images. (tr) Artville. **12** (br) © Radius Images/Alamy. **13** (bl) © David Young-Wolff/PhotoEdit. (tl) Marmion. Image from BigStockPhoto.com. (tr) © Radius Images/ Alamy. (t) ULTRA.F/Jupiter Images. (br) © Janine Wiedel Photolibrary/Alamy. **14** (bkgd) © Simon Marcus/Corbis. (tl) John Lund/Sam Diephuis/Blend Images/Getty Images. **15** (tl) © Rob/Fotolia. (tl) Lisa F. Young/LisaFX Photographic Designs. Image from BigStockPhoto.com. (tr) © Michael Newman/PhotoEdit. (tr) © David Young-Wolff/PhotoEdit. (cl) © Bonnie Kamin/PhotoEdit. (cl) Jupiter Images. (cr) © Kayte Deioma/PhotoEdit. (cr) ©Monartdesign.com/Fotolia. (bl) Rob Marmion. Image from BigStockPhoto.com. (bc) © David Young-Wolff/ PhotoEdit. (br) Jason Stitt. Image from BigStockPhoto. com. (br) Rob Marmion. Image from BigStockPhoto. com. **16** (tl) ©JUPITERIMAGES/Thinkstock/Alamy. (tr) © Cindy Charles/PhotoEdit Inc. (b) © Design Pics Inc./ Alamy. **17** (tl) Ariel Skelley/Blend Images/Getty Images. (tr) © Spencer Grant/PhotoEdit Inc. (c) © David Young-Wolff/PhotoEdit Inc. **18** (tl) Masterfile (Royalty-Free Div.). (br) Amos Morgan/Jupiter Images. **19** (b) Feverpitch Photography/iStockphoto. (tr) aabejoniStockphoto. **20** (cr) sx70/iStockphoto. (bl) Tritooth/Dreamstime LLC. **21** (cr) aabejon/iStockphotos. (tr) Artville. **24** (c) (c) Garry Wade/Jupiter Images. (bkgd) © Image copyright Chris Bradshaw, 2009. Used under license from Shutterstock.com. (cl) Robert Nicholas/ Jupiter Images. **25** (bl) © W. Cody/CORBIS. (bl) © W. Cody/CORBIS. (cr) © W. Cody/CORBIS. **26** (bl) © UpperCut Images/Alamy. (c) © Blend Images/Alamy. (bkgd) © Image copyright Andrey Armyagov, 2009. Used under license from Shutterstock.com. **27** (bc) © Image copyright Ajay Bhaskar, 2009. Used under license from Shutterstock.com. (tr) John Lund/Sam Diephuis/ Jupiter Images. **28** (tl) © Image copyright Rob Marmion, 2009. Used under license from Shutterstock.com. (bl) © chris Bott/Alamy. (cl) Rolf Bruderer/Photo Library. **29** (tr) NGSP. (b) Scott B. Rosen/BSG/NGSP. (b) © Andrey Khrolenok/Fotolia. **30** (bl) MBPHOTO/iStockphoto. (cr) Jose Luis Pelaez Inc/Getty Images. (bl) Ajphotos/ Dreamstime.com. (bl) © Image copyright michaeljung, 2009. Used under license from Shutterstock.com. **31** (tcl) Liz Garza Williams. (bcl) Ron Chapple Stock/Photo Library. (cr) Artville. (tr) AlterYourReality/iStockphoto. (bl) Jack Hollingsworth/Jackhollinsworth.com, LLC. Image from BigStockPhoto.com. (tl) Lancelot/Photo Library. **35** (br) © Olivier Asselin/Alamy. (cl) © Jeff Greenberg/PhotoEdit. (cl) © Sarah Hadley/Alamy. (tr) © Charles O. Cecil/Alamy. (tr) © Jeff Greenberg/PhotoEdit. **36** (bl) Comstock Images/Jupiter Images. (tl) © Philippe S. Giraud/Terres du Sud/Sygma/Corbisis. All Rights Reserved. (r) Masterfile (Royalty-Free Div.). **37** (tr) Jose Inc/PhotoLibrary. (cr) (c) ballyscanlon/Jupiter Images. (br) RFR/Alamy. **38** (bl) MetaTools. (bcl) NGSP. (bc) SuperStock. (bcr) © devon. Image from BigStockPhoto. com. (br) Jupiter Images. (tc) Jupiter Images. (bkgd) © amana images inc./Alamy. (c) Getty Images. **39** (bl) Siede Preis/Jupiter Images. (tr) radarreklama/Fotolia. (cl) © devon. Image from BigStockPhoto.com. (cl) Stephen Rees. Image from BigStockPhoto.com. (cr) Getty Images. (cr) Lai Leng Yiap. Image from BigStockPhoto.com. (bl) Getty Images. (bl) Getty Images. (bl) Feng Yu/Fotolia. **42** (bl) © Image copyright Gelpi, 2009. Used under license from Shutterstock.com. (tl) PhotoAlto/Alamy. (c) Scott B. Rosen/BSG/NGSP. **43** (b) Bruce Laurance/Jupiter Images. (t) ©Suto Norbert/Fotolia. **44** (tl) Andersen Ross/Blend Images/Getty Images. (bl) lisafx/iStockphoto. (cl) © Skynesher/Dreamstime.com. (cr) © Sean Locke/ iStockphoto. (tr) Arekmalang/Dreamstime LLC. (tc) Jupiter Images. (c) © devon. Image from BigStockPhoto. com. (bc) Getty Images. (cl) Amos Morgan/Jupiter Images. **45** (br) © Image copyright Jacek Chabraszewski, 2009. Used under license from Shutterstock.com. (tr) Jupiter Images. (b) MetaTools. **46** (cr) NGSP. **47** (bkgd) Kablonk!/Photo Library. **48** (bkgd) © Jose Manuel Gelpi/ Fotolia. (tl) © Image copyright Gelpi, 2009. Used under license from Shutterstock.com. (tl) © Gelpi/Dreamstime. com. (cl) Lai Leng Yiap. Image from BigStockPhoto.com. (cl) © devon. Image from BigStockPhoto.com. (cl) Getty Images. (cl) SuperStock. (cl) NGSP. (cl) MetaTools. (cl) Getty Images. (cl) Photodisc/Alamy. (cl) Jupiter Images. (cl) © Robyn Mackenzie. Image from BigStockPhoto. com. (cl) Getty Images. (t) Getty Images. (cl) Getty Images. (cl) © Garycookson/Dreamstime.com. **49** (bcr) © devon. Image from BigStockPhoto.com. (tcr) SuperStock. (t) NGSP. (t) MetaTools. (tcl) Getty Images. (cl) Photodisc/Alamy. (bcl) Jupiter Images. (bl) 2008 © Robyn Mackenzie. Image from BigStockPhoto.com. (br) Getty Images. **50** (tc) Digital Vision/Getty Images. (bl) © Spencer Grant/PhotoEdit. (bcl) Dorling KindersleyGetty Images. (bcr) © Bill Aron/PhotoEdit. (br) Jupiter Images. **51** (tl) Photodisc/Alamy. (tcl) Jupiter Images. (bcl) Dorling Kindersley/Getty Images. (tr) © Steve Skjold/ Alamy. (tcr) © Spencer Grant/PhotoEdit. (bcr) © David Young-Wolff/PhotoEdit. (bl) © Bill Aron/PhotoEdit. **54** (tl) radarreklama/Fotolia. (tr) Kimberly Reinick/Fotolia. (bl) Getty Images. (br) Pedro Diaz/Fotolia. (tcr) NGSP. (bcl) Javier Pazo. Image from BigStockPhoto.com. (bcr) NGSP. (tl) Getty Images. **55** (tr) © Glenjones/ Dreamstime.com. (b) © Michael Newman/PhotoEdit. (tl) elnur/Fotolia. (tr) Glenjones/Dreamstime.com. **56** (cr) Comstock/Jupiter Images. (bl) © Image copyright Cynthia Farmer, 2009. Used under license from Shutterstock.com. **60** (cl) ©2009 Getty Images. (cr) © Lisa F. Young/iStockphoto. (bkgd t) © Image copyright Rob Byron, 2009. Used under license from Shutterstock. com. (br) © RFR/Alamy. (bkgd) BSG. (bl) © Visions of America, LLC/Alamy. (bl) © Visions of America, LLC/ Alamy. (br) © Kathy deWitt/Alamy. **61** (bkgd) RFR/Alamy. (cr) Andre Jenny/Alamy. **62** (bkgd) ©Syracuse Newspapers/Stephen Cannerelli/The Image Works. (br) © William Whitehurst/CORBIS. **63** (bkgd t) © John Cooper/Alamy. (bl) Steve VanHorn. Image from BigStockPhoto.com. **64** (tl) © Image copyright Thomas M Perkins, 2009. Used under license from Shutterstock. com. (tr) © Paul Burns/Corbis. (bcr) Stockbyte/Jupiter Images. (tc) Big Cheese Photo/Jupiter Images. (c) © Glenjones/Dreamstime.com. (tcl) Getty Images. **65** (b) Rob/Fotolia. (bl) © Kathy deWitt/Alamy. (tr) Masterfile (Royalty-Free Div.). **66** (cr) Inti St Clair/Jupiter Images. **68** (bkgd) Spike Mafford/Getty Images. (cl) NGSP. **71** (tcr) © Peter Steiner/Alamy. (t) © Image copyright roadk, 2009. Used under license from Shutterstock.com. **72** (r) (c) Image Source/Jupiter Images. (bl) Radius Images/ Jupiter Images. (tl) © Image copyright Sandra Cunningham, 2009. Used under license from Shutterstock.com. **73** (tr) Beau Lark/Fancy/Jupiter Images. (br) © Gary Conner/PhotoEdit. **74** (cr) © Darius Ramazani/Corbis. (bkgd) ©Onidji/Fotolia. (bl) pkruger. Image from BigStockPhoto.com. (b) pkruger. Image from BigStockPhoto.com. (br) pkruger. Image from BigStockPhoto.com. **76** (cl) © hartlandmartin. Image from BigStockPhoto.com. (c) 2008 ©volk65. Image from BigStockPhoto.com. (cr) © intelwebs/Fotolia. (bl) © HP_Photo/Fotolia. (bc) ©JUPITERIMAGES/Comstock Images/Alamy. (tl) pkruger. Image from BigStockPhoto. com. (tl) pkruger. Image from BigStockPhoto.com. (tc) pkruger. Image from BigStockPhoto.com. (tc) pkruger. Image from BigStockPhoto.com. (tc) pkruger. Image from BigStockPhoto.com. (tr) pkruger. Image from BigStockPhoto.com. (tr) pkruger. Image from BigStockPhoto.com. **77** (tl) © lofoto/Dreamstime.com. (bcl) © Mayangsari/Dreamstime.com. (bl) Jupiterimages. (tr) © Kwame Zikomo/SuperStock. (cr) Jack Hollingsworth/Jupiter Images. (tcl) Kindra Clineff/ Photo Library. (bcr) Masterfile (Royalty-Free Div.). (tr) pkruger. Image from BigStockPhoto.com. (cr) pkruger. Image from BigStockPhoto.com. (br) pkruger. Image from BigStockPhoto.com. **78** (cl) Onidji/Fotolia. (cr) ©JUPITERIMAGES/Creatas/Alamy. (bl) 81A Productions/ Photo Library. (br) ©JUPITERIMAGES/Creatas/Alamy. **79** (br) © Image Source/SuperStock. (tr) © Corbis Super RF/ Alamy. **80** (cr) Scott B. Rosen/BSG/NGSP. (bl) © Image copyright Gilian McGregor, 2009. Used under license from Shutterstock.com. **81** (tl) Nick Koudis/Photodisc/ Getty Images. (tl) Janis Christie/Photodisc/Getty Images. (t) Artville. (tr) Jupiterimages. (tr) Artville. (tl) Photodisc/Getty Images. (tcl) SuperStock. (bcl) Getty Images. (bl) Liz Garza Williams. (tc) Artville. (c) Liz Garza Williams. (bc) Artville. (bc) Artville. (tr) Artville. (tcr) Getty Images. (bcr) John Paul Endress. (br) John Paul Endress. **82** (br) DougSchneiderPhoto/iStockphoto. (bl) pkruger. Image from BigStockPhoto.com. (tl) © Image copyright Ales Nowak, 2009. Used under license from Shutterstock.com. (bl) © Image copyright Ales Nowak, 2009. Used under license from Shutterstock.com. **83** (analog clocks) pkruger. Image from BigStockPhoto. com. **84** (c) Andersen Ross/Jupiter Images. (bl) DonNichols/iStockphoto. (br) © Monkeybusinessimages/Dreamstime.com. (cr) Getty Images. (b) © Claudia Wiens/Alamy. **85** (b) © Claudia Wiens/Alamy. (t) © Monkeybusinessimages/ Dreamstime.com. (c) JGI/Jupiter Images. (bl) Masterfile. (cl) © Simon Jarratt/Corbis. (cr) Liquidlibrary/Getty Images/Jupiter Images. (tl) Terry Vine/Blend Images/ Getty Images. (bl) Arthur Tilley/Jupiter Images. **86** (t) © Paula27/Dreamstime.com. (b) © SuperStock RF/ SuperStock. **87** (b) © cultura/Corbis. (tr) © Onidji/ Fotolia. **88** (bl) © D. Hurst/Alamy. (cr) © Blend Images/ Alamy. **89** (cr) © Jackmicro/Dreamstime. (tr) Artville. **92** (c) © Michael Newman/PhotoEdit. (c) © Bonnie Kamin/ PhotoEdit. (br) © David R. Frazier Photolibrary, Inc./ Alamy. (bl) Aaron Haupt/Photo Researchers. (bcl) Copyright © Billy E. Barnes/PhotoEdit. (bcr) © Kinn Deacon/Alamy. (c) © Fancy/Alamy. **93** (tl) Masterfile (Royalty-Free Div.). (bl) © Martin Mayer/Alamy. **94** (tl) Aaron Haupt/Photo Researchers. (bl) © Picture Contact/ Alamy. **95** (bl) © Michael Newman/PhotoEdit. (tl) © Ian Shaw/Alamy. **96** (tl) © Michael Chamberlin/Fotolia. (bl) ©SuperStock. **97** (bl) Ryan McVay/Jupiter Images. (tl) © Wolfram Schroll/Corbis. (cl) © Corbis Super RF/Alamy. (tl) © Michael Newman/PhotoEdit. **98** (t) Masterfile (Royalty-Free Div.). (b) Tanya Constantine/Blend Images/Jupiter Images. **99** (br) © Image copyright Rob Marmion, 2009. Used under license from Shutterstock. com. **100** (tl) Image Source/Jupiter Images. (cl) pixdeluxe/iStockphoto. (bl) Andersen Ross/Jupiter Images. (tr) (c) Jupiterimages. (cr) © Blend Images/ Alamy. (br) perkmeup/iStockphoto. **101** (b) © Image